"This work brings ————— ..... contemporary defender of the resurrection and the foremost atheist of the 20th century. While the style is warm and conversational, this book is all meat and no fluff. Baggett's assessment of the debate alone is worth the price of the book. I highly recommend this to all who wish to defend the historical credibility of the resurrection of Jesus. The debate is a model of civility."

J.P. MORELAND, Distinguished Professor of Philosophy, Talbot School of Theology, and coauthor of *In Search of a Confident Faith*

"As a reader of *Did the Resurrection Happen? A Conversation with Gary Habermas and Antony Flew,* I experienced the rare pleasure of eavesdropping on a rigorous discussion between close friends. While they persist in their strong disagreement over a variety of substantive issues, Habermas and Flew never fail to argue with charity and humor. This posture gives the book a warm and congenial flavor. It is a great read for anyone interested in philosophy, in the resurrection or in how best to engage in significant debate."

GREGORY E. GANSSLE, Rivendell Institute, department of philosophy, Yale University

"This book is a dialogue between the leading expert on Jesus' resurrection and the most influential atheist philosopher of the late twentieth century. No fluff. No insults. This is an intelligent and friendly exchange of ideas among two giants in their field who have arrived at radically different views of what happened to Jesus 2,000 years ago."

MICHAEL R. LICONA, director of apologetics, North American Mission Board

"This book offers not only a lively exchange on Jesus' resurrection between Habermas and Flew. The section on Flew's pilgrimage to belief in God and the excellent analysis by Baggett help both round out the dialogue as well as provide much food for philosophical and theological thought. A superb resource on the resurrection!"

PAUL COPAN, professor and Pledger Family Chair of Philosophy and Ethics, Palm Beach Atlantic University, West Palm Beach, Florida

"A lively conversation about the most important question in the history, and for the future, of the world. Habermas's compelling answers to Flew's questions awaken hope within me. The resurrection and vindication of Christ frees us from the fear of death, and for true life, now and forever. I wish this book for all of us, especially skeptics who are also thinkers."

KELLY MONROE KULLBERG, founder and director of project development, The Veritas Forum, author of *Finding God Beyond Harvard: The Quest for Veritas,* and editor of *Finding God at Harvard: Spiritual Journeys of Thinking Christians*

"David Baggett has skillfully edited an engaging and warm-hearted debate between Gary Habermas and Antony Flew, two of the world's foremost philosophers and thinkers, the former a Christian and apologist and the latter a well-known atheist who recently has embraced deism. Their debate centers on the very essence of Christian faith—the resurrection of Jesus Christ. This is a great book. I recommend it enthusiastically."

CRAIG A. EVANS, Payzant Distinguished Professor of New Testament, Acadia Divinity College

"The conversation between Habermas and Flew has been a fascinating one at the highest levels of philosophical reflection. This book beautifully chronicles that dialogue in a way that is clear for those not versed in philosophy. The book will cause you to sit and ponder. That is a compliment enough, but more than that you will learn how two competing worldviews should interact with each other—and that is a real gift."

DARRELL BOCK, Dallas Theological Seminary

A Conversation with
Gary Habermas and Antony Flew

DID THE RESURRECTION HAPPEN

EDITED BY **DAVID BAGGETT**

IVP Books

An imprint of InterVarsity Press
Downers Grove, Illinois

InterVarsity Press
P.O. Box 1400, Downers Grove, IL 60515-1426
ivpress.com
email@ivpress.com

InterVarsity Press® is the book-publishing division of InterVarsity Christian Fellowship/USA®, a movement of students and faculty active on campus at hundreds of universities, colleges and schools of nursing in the United States of America, and a member movement of the International Fellowship of Evangelical Students. For information about local and regional activities, visit intervarsity.org.

Scripture quotations, unless otherwise noted, are from the New Revised Standard Version of the Bible, copyright 1989 by the Division of Christian Education of the National Council of the Churches of Christ in the USA. Used by permission. All rights reserved.

The article "My Pilgrimage from Atheism to Theism: A Discussion Between Antony Flew and Gary Habermas," by Antony Flew and Gary R. Habermas, originally appeared in Philosophia Christi 6, no. 2 (2004): 197-211, and the article "Antony Flew's Deism Revisited: A Review Essay on There Is a God," by Antony Flew and Gary R. Habermas, first appeared in Philosophia Christi 9, no. 2 (2007): 431-41. Both appear courtesy of the Evangelical Philosophical Society (www.epsociety.org). Used by permission.

Design: Cindy Kiple

Images: Richard Ross/Getty Images

ISBN 978-0-8308-3718-2

Printed in the United States of America ∞

 As a member of the Green Press Initiative, InterVarsity Press is committed to protecting the environment and to the responsible use of natural resources. To learn more, visit greenpressinitiative.org.

Library of Congress Cataloging-in-Publication Data

Habermas, Gary R.
   Did the Resurrection happen?: a conversation with Gary Habermas and
   Antony Flew / edited by David Baggett.
      p. cm.
   Includes bibliographical references (p.   ) and index.
   ISBN 978-0-8308-3718-2 (pbk.: alk. paper)
   1. Jesus Christ—Resurrection. 2. Religious disputations. I. Flew,
   Antony, 1923-. II. Baggett, David. III. Title.
   BT482.H32 2009
   232.9'7—dc22

                                                                      2009000424

P   24   23   22   21   20   19   18   17   16   15   14   13   12   11   10   9   8   7   6   5   4   3   2
Y   34   33   32   31   30   29   28   27   26   25   24   23   22   21   20   19   18   17   16   15

To Jerry Walls,
teacher, colleague, mentor, friend

CONTENTS

PREFACE

THE VERITAS FORUM EXISTS TO CREATE discussions exploring life's hardest questions and the relevance of Jesus Christ to all of life. The conversation which forms the basis of this book is an inspiring example of just that—not a debate or a dialogue where one side seeks to triumph over another, but instead a joint exploration of one of the ultimate questions of humanity—the resurrection of Jesus Christ.

When I first saw the video of this Veritas Forum event held at Cal Poly, San Luis Obispo in 2003, it felt as if I were eavesdropping on a private chat between old friends. In Antony Flew and Gary Habermas we see two men driven not by ideologies or agendas but by a shared passion for truth and a common respect for the response the truth demands. It was our honor to host such a winsome, open, articulate encounter embodying what a search for truth looks like.

Moreover, although this dialogue about ultimate truth was in the university setting, their search for meaning is one that draws us together in every stage of life. Many students and other seekers of truth will find in Dr. Flew a brilliant and humble once-atheist scholar whose journey and outlook resonates with their own. His position is in stark contrast to the often hostile, alienating polemics of recent years which unfortunately all but monopolize the discussion. And those of us who are followers of Jesus should also remember that this one night's conversation emerged from an eighteen-year friendship.

That said, many envisioned and labored to create the occasion for this event, and we owe them our gratitude. In particular, Jamey Pappas, longtime advisor for The Veritas Forum at Cal Poly and director of SLOCrusade, led a team of students and staff in planning this and many other Veritas events. Mike Swanson was the student planning team director that year. And Ted and Ashley Callahan led the Veritas national movement that supported Jamey and other teams around the country from 2003-2005. And of course, special thanks to Dr. Flew and Dr. Habermas for allowing us to invite many more participants into their conversation in print.

May the pages that follow lead you on your own exploration of true life in the person and story of Jesus Christ.

Daniel Cho
Executive Director
The Veritas Forum

ACKNOWLEDGMENTS

IT'S OUR PLEASURE TO THANK the various people who helped us with this book. We are deeply appreciative of Daniel Cho and The Veritas Forum for conferring permission to publish this dialogue, and not just permission, but also their enthusiastic support. Thanks to Dan as well for writing the preface. The project owes much to Craig Hazen and Joe Gorra and *Philosophia Christi* for giving their permission to reprint two of Gary's articles and providing us electronic copies of them to facilitate publication. The work these philosophers are doing at *Philosophia Christi* is top-notch and of great benefit to the church today. Many thanks to Al Hsu and the good folks at InterVarsity Press for believing in this project and seeing it through to completion. And special thanks to various colleagues and friends for their support and help, including their critiques and challenges: John Azar, Greg Bassham, Mark Foreman, Don Fowler, Bill Irwin, Tim McGrew, Tom Morris, Thom Provenzola, Bruce Russell and especially Jerry Walls. Many thanks to a terrific research assistant, Steve Hudson, who transcribed most of the debate, and to Wesley Grubb for doing the remaining portion. And thanks to Ryan Andrews for his work compiling the index.

INTRODUCTION

A Man, a Friendship and an Argument

David Baggett

THIS BOOK IS ABOUT A MAN, a friendship and an argument. The man is Dr. Antony Flew, the friendship is between Flew and Dr. Gary Habermas, and the argument concerns whether or not the resurrection of Jesus really happened.

Flew is one of the foremost analytic philosophers and perhaps the most famous philosophical atheist of the twentieth century who, to the surprise of many, left atheism behind in 2004, declaring himself a theist, more accurately a Deist. His conversion caught international attention. Even Jay Leno joked about it in his monologue one night.

Flew is a longtime friend of Habermas, a garrulous and gregarious Christian philosopher who is arguably the world's leading expert on the historicity of the resurrection of Jesus. Over the course of their twenty-five-year dialogue, Flew and Habermas, their differences notwithstanding, have forged a friendship that's a real model for how friendships can thrive despite disagreements. In a context like today, where animus and invective often pervade what passes for dialogue between atheists and believers, or between theists of various stripes, we could all learn something from the graciousness and warmth of these two men.

"To the Ancients," C. S. Lewis once wrote, "friendship seemed the happiest and most fully human of all loves; the crown of life and the school of virtue."[1] Lewis went on to say,

> Friendship arises out of mere Companionship when two or
> more of the companions discover that they have in common
> some insight or interest or even taste which the others do not
> share and which, till that moment, each believed to be his own
> unique treasure (or burden). The typical expression of opening
> Friendship would be something like, "What? You too? I thought
> I was the only one."[2]

Of friendship, William James once wrote to Wendell Holmes, "I
have grown into the belief that friendship . . . is about the highest joy
of earth and that a man's rank in the general scale is well indicated
by his capacity for it."[3]

Blaise Pascal once lamented that people spend too much time
thinking about the trivial and too little time thinking about the sub-
lime. In a day when superficialities mesmerize attention and occupy
our time, Flew and Habermas have built a friendship discussing matters of substance. They met in 1985 at a conference featuring a dialogue between theists and atheists, and immediately formed a bond.
Over dinner at that same conference they planned a debate in Virginia later that year on the topic of the historical case for the resurrection of Jesus. Flew was one of the world's leading experts on miracles and David Hume. Habermas was already, even then in his
mid-thirties, on his way to becoming the world's leading expert on
the resurrection. The event was bound to be a special one.

And special it was! Moderated by Dr. Terry Miethe, the debate and
subsequent dialogue (between Habermas, Flew, Miethe and Dr. David Beck) covered two days: May 2 and 3, 1985. Three thousand people attended, and two five-person panels of experts professionally

---

[1]C. S. Lewis, *The Four Loves* (New York: Harcourt Brace, 1960), p. 87.
[2]Ibid., p. 96.
[3]John J. McDermott, gen. ed., *The Correspondence of William James*, ed. Ignas K. Skrup-
skelis, Elizabeth Berkeley and Frederick H. Burkhardt (Charlottesville: University of
Virginia Press, 1992-2004), 4:300.

judged the debate—one panel composed of philosophers, another of professional debate judges. This group of ten represented a range of worldviews and served on the faculties of American colleges and universities, such as the University of Virginia and George Mason University. Miethe would later publish the proceedings of this debate in *Did Jesus Rise from the Dead?*[4] He invited Wolfhart Pannenberg, Charles Hartshorne and J. I. Packer to offer written replies, all of which are included in the book. Miethe also included a final essay by Habermas, whom judges had chosen as the winner by a 7-2 margin (with one draw).

Over the next twenty years, despite the ocean separating them physically and ideologically, Habermas and Flew continued to correspond and chat. "Over the years," Habermas says, "Tony and I also exchanged dozens of letters. In our many phone calls, we could just as easily discuss the British or American educational systems, or any number of other topics."[5] More recently, at the triennial C. S. Lewis conference "Oxbridge," Habermas added,

> Tony has caused me to do a lot of thinking regarding the role of friendship. We've been good friends for a long time, and I think there's something to be said for friendship between believers and unbelievers. Perhaps this is another side of the legacy of C. S. Lewis—that friends can dialogue and everyone does not have to agree as a precondition for mutual appreciation. This is an aspect of tolerance at its best, that good friends can discuss what's going on in the news, whether serious or not.[6]

---

[4]Gary R. Habermas and Antony G. N. Flew, *Did Jesus Rise from the Dead? The Resurrection Debate*, ed. Terry L. Miethe (San Francisco: Harper & Row, 1987).

[5]Gary R. Habermas and Antony Flew, "From Atheism to Deism: A Conversation Between Antony Flew and Gary R. Habermas," in *C. S. Lewis as Philosopher: Truth, Goodness and Beauty*, ed. Jerry L. Walls, David Baggett and Gary Habermas (Downers Grove, Ill.: IVP Academic, 2008), p. 40.

[6]Ibid., p. 46.

At that same conference I met Flew and Habermas for the first time. I loved the study in contrasts. Flew is a very quiet, almost bashful, extremely soft-spoken Englishman, while Habermas is an extroverted, ebullient American. When I first met Habermas in the dining hall of St. Catherine's College, Oxford University—after realizing I had been speaking with his wife, Eileen, already—my first thought was, "It's the resurrection guy!" (My second was, "Lee Strobel was right! He really *does* look more like a nightclub bouncer than an ivory tower academic."[7]) Seeing their friendship up close and personal is indeed inspiring, for it's a model of philosophical dialogue at its best.

So in the spirit of continuing the dialogue, this book is likely the final installment of their ongoing discussion about the resurrection of Jesus. After the 1985 debate, there would be two more: their second was on the Inspiration Network in April 2000 and later on the *John Ankerberg Show*, published as *Resurrected? An Atheist and Theist Dialogue.*[8] Their third debate was in January 2003 at California Polytechnic State University, San Luis Obispo, an event sponsored by The Veritas Forum. The first part of this book is the transcript of that debate and therefore marks the culmination of the formal part of their dialogue, which carries on informally even now.

After this third debate, Habermas describes one particular moment in the hotel as they were parting: "I got off the elevator, but Tony was going to an upper floor in the hotel. . . . Then there was sort of a surrealistic experience for me. As I got off the elevator, I thrust my hand back through the open door to shake his hand and said, 'When you become a Christian, I want to be the first one to know.' And [Flew] said, 'I think you've earned that right.'"[9]

Shortly after that debate, Flew informed Habermas he was consid-

---

[7]Lee Strobel, *Case for Christ: A Journalist's Personal Investigation of the Evidence for Jesus* (Grand Rapids: Zondervan, 1998), p. 226.

[8]Gary R. Habermas and Antony G. N. Flew, *Resurrected? An Atheist and Theist Dialogue,* ed. John F. Ankerberg (Lanham, Md.: Rowman and Littlefield, 2005).

[9]Habermas and Flew, "From Atheism to Deism," p. 46.

ering theism, and the following January, one year to the month after this debate, Flew admitted that reading Aristotle had inclined him further toward theism. He thought that was where the evidence was leading him, and he was willing to follow it. He realized he had come to believe that God, in fact, exists.

They soon taped a lengthy conversation, had it transcribed and worked on developing a manuscript chronicling Flew's conversion (to theism, not Christianity). About two weeks before the article was due to appear, reports of Flew's change of mind hit the news, featuring titles like "Thinking Straighter: Why the World's Most Famous Atheist Now Believes in God," and, Habermas's favorite, "Flew the Coup." The edited transcript of their own discussion about Flew's ideological shift was published in early 2005 with the title "My Pilgrimage from Atheism to Theism" and is reprinted here.

Flew further described his intellectual pilgrimage in his 2007 book, written with Roy Abraham Varghese, *There Is a God: How the World's Most Notorious Atheist Changed His Mind.*[10] Habermas has written a review essay of this book, which is reprinted here as well, with the gracious permission of *Philosophia Christi*.

Flew's intellectual honesty, his willingness to change in response to evidence, and his friendship with Habermas are compelling and inspiring stories, but both Flew and Habermas would insist that we look beyond them to the questions and issues that drew them together as friends in the first place. So, ultimately and most importantly, this book is about an argument. To a philosopher, *argument* is not a dirty word or a thing to be avoided. It involves no raised voices or hair-pulling, at least not paradigmatically and not just because so many philosophers are bald. Rightly understood, argument is a reasonable assessment of the evidence. It is an attempt to figure out what's true on the basis of the facts we have at our disposal. Habermas has constructed just such an argument for the resurrection.

---

[10]Antony Flew with Roy Abraham Varghese, *There Is a God: How the World's Most Notorious Atheist Changed His Mind* (New York: HarperCollins, 2007).

Since this book represents the third and likely last debate between these two thinkers on this question of questions, and since Flew has now become a theist, it's an appropriate time to take stock. So in the final section, "Resurrection Matters: Assessing the Habermas/Flew Discussion," I discuss this fascinating twenty-some-year dialogue between these two gentlemen. I summarize the argument, dividing it into two parts—the evidence and the inference on the basis of that evidence—and look at the evidence and the inference from both a sympathetic and a critical perspective. I don't presume to speak for anyone but myself in offering the appraisals I do, so readers must decide for themselves what to think of it all. After identifying the salient philosophical aspects of the argument, I return again to Flew, assessing where he is in his intellectual pilgrimage and what might happen from here.

The resurrection of Jesus is surely one of the most important topics philosophers of religion can discuss. Two distinguishable issues here are often conflated: the event itself and the argument for rational belief in the event on the basis of historical evidence. Christian theology itself says that unless the event itself transpired, Christian faith is in vain. The resurrection has always been at the absolute center of what Christianity teaches. If the resurrection didn't happen, Christianity is simply false. Clearly this is the import of the apostle Paul's saying with point-blank precision and in unequivocal terms that if the resurrection didn't happen, Christian hope is empty; that if Christ isn't risen from the dead, Christians are of all people most miserable (1 Cor 15:19). If the resurrection did happen, Christianity is very plausibly taken to be true.

This book examines the historical case for rational belief in the resurrection, which is a slightly different matter. It's tempting to say that, if the historical case fails, then Christianity is false, but this isn't exactly right. Plenty of historical events have taken place without our ability today to establish that they did. An effective historical case for the resurrection makes rational belief in the resurrection possible, without ensuring that the event happened. The absence of such a case doesn't, however, mean the event didn't transpire, but it would mean that rational belief in the resurrection would have to derive from other sources.

William Lane Craig, for example, argues that we can come to know the truth that the resurrection happened both historically and in a more personal way, through something like the testimony of the Holy Spirit. Alvin Plantinga, a Reformed epistemologist, argues similarly that the great doctrines of Christianity may well be known nonevidentially and more directly. However, even if this is the case, the historical evidence should still be considered. For if such a case can be made, surely it should be made. Paul, among others, clearly intended to make such an appeal. Your personal conviction about the matter may be good for you, but it doesn't do anyone else any favors.

Careful assessment of the evidence is important in a further regard. No small number of religious believers today disparage the role of reason and evidence, not because they're intelligent Reformed epistemologists, but because they're fideists. For them faith is, by definition, blind. Looking at the evidence actually runs counter to real faith, which has as its defining mark an absence of evidence or a leap of blind faith against the available evidence.

This Enlightenment and vulgarized Kierkegaardian notion of religious faith as devoid of rationality is a radical departure from both biblical faith, rightly understood, and the view of the greatest Christian minds through the centuries—from Anselm to Augustine to Aquinas. Faith is not believing what you know ain't so, as Mark Twain once put it, nor is it inconsistent with evidence. Rightly understood, and quite to the contrary, it's more like trust in a husband or wife to be faithful. It's a choice based on solid evidence, trust in the character of this person, confidence that he or she will do what was promised. Biblical faith is unswerving trust in God to be faithful to his promises and character; it's not blind trust that he exists, but an abiding and principled sense of assurance both that he exists and that he is faithful, despite our own unfaithfulness.

For Christians, a strong historical case for the resurrection can provide a powerful antidote to the pervasive view today, held by many believers and unbelievers, that religion in general and Christianity in particular isn't about evidence, but about (blind) faith. Nothing could be further from the truth—or more effective at rendering Christian thought intellectually irrelevant.

So, without further ado, let's listen in on the last official chapter of Habermas and Flew discussing a matter that truly matters.

PART I

2003 Resurrection Debate Between Antony Flew and Gary Habermas

California Polytechnic University, San Luis Obispo, January 3, 2003
Moderated by Dr. Joe Lynch

THIS EVENING, THE QUESTION BEFORE US is this: Did Jesus of Nazareth rise from the dead? It's a really important question. The apostle Paul is quoted as saying that, basically, if Jesus didn't rise from the dead, then his faith and the faith of all other Christians is in vain. So it's really quite an important question.

This evening we have with us some of the world's most prominent scholars, so it's very exciting. We also have with us Dr. Joe Lynch of the philosophy department here at Cal Poly, who will be serving as moderator this evening.

Let me explain a bit of the format for the evening. Last year we had a debate on this very same question. This year we're having more of an informal, or perhaps formal, discussion. Dr. Lynch as moderator is going to prompt these two gentlemen with questions and is going to serve to facilitate discussion of the question before us. A little background on Dr. Lynch: Dr. Lynch, once again, is a philosophy professor here at Cal Poly. He teaches classes ranging from philosophical classics to philosophy of religion to Asian philosophy to philosophy of mind and more. So he's very well qualified to be with us this evening. He earned his Ph.D. in philosophy from Claremont and studied with the likes of John Hick and others. I'll let him say more about these gentlemen this evening, so if you would help me welcome Dr. Lynch.

HISTORICAL EVIDENCE FOR THE CRUCIFIXION, DEATH, BURIAL AND RESURRECTION OF JESUS

Moderator: I would like to introduce to you these eminent philosophers who are with us tonight. On my left is Antony Flew. If you took philosophy of religion with me, you would read him every quarter. He is a very well-known British philosopher, and I learned earlier today that he was influential in intelligence in the RAF [Royal Air Force]. A very fun story. But he's published innumerable articles in all areas of philosophy, and relevant for our area of discussion, he's published works like *God, Freedom, and Immortality* and *Atheistic Humanism*. So you can guess what side of the discussion he might be on by that.

On my right is the chair of philosophy at Liberty University, back in my home state of Virginia, Gary Habermas. Professor Habermas has published in many philosophical journals and books, and his main areas of specialization deal with philosophical issues surrounding the resurrection. So I look forward to a good discussion, and later on you are going to have a chance to participate and ask your questions.

So, in order to get things started now, on the screen before you today you can see a title there that says "The Known Historical Facts." These are supposed to be facts that we can hook in so that we can have an area of agreement because, if we don't have an area of agreement, then it is hard to have any discussion; people will just be talking past each other. I'm going to go through these, and then I'll first throw the door open to Professor Flew and ask for his reactions and, with any luck at all, a discussion will ensue.

1. Jesus died by crucifixion.

2. He was buried.

3. The death of Jesus caused the disciples to despair and lose hope, believing that his life was ended.

4. Although not as widely accepted, many scholars hold that the tomb in which Jesus was buried was discovered to be empty just a few days later.

5. The disciples had experiences they believed were the literal appearances of the risen Jesus.

6. The disciples were transformed from doubters who were afraid to identify themselves with Jesus to bold proclaimers of his death and resurrection.

7. This message was the center of preaching in the early church.

8. This message was especially proclaimed in Jerusalem, where Jesus died and was buried shortly before.

9. As a result of this teaching, the church was born and grew.

10. Sunday became the primary day of worship.

11. James, who had been a skeptic, was converted to the faith when he also believed that he had seen the resurrected Jesus.

12. A few years later, Paul was converted by an experience that he likewise believed to be an appearance of the risen Jesus.[1]

So, perhaps now, Professor Flew, you could say what areas you agree or disagree in?

Flew: Well, crucified, yes of course, we have abundant evidence for that. Dead? I think so, but wait a moment, because Pilate, who undoubtedly had experience of crucifixions, was surprised that Jesus was finally dead at that time and then he was taken down. Now, in view of other things that have become known now, there are possibilities of some sort of revival.

The next thing, surely, do we have evidence of the actual burial?

---

[1]See Gary R. Habermas, *The Historical Jesus: Ancient Evidence for the Life of Christ* (Joplin, Mo.: College Press, 1996), p. 158.

Yes, we have evidence that Joseph of Arimathea was proposing to bury Jesus, and we also have evidence of the tomb being empty. But what we don't have evidence of is its being occupied.

A rather different line I want to take up later, granted that he rose from the dead and was moving around, is this: what is the next stage? Presumably he's not buried again; he presumably goes up to heaven. Now, what is involved in this? Is the body supposed to rise up and somehow disappear? I don't think we have any information about what is even expected to have happened there. To complete a resurrection, surely we've got to have a death and presumably an actual burial and then another stage about which nothing clear seems to have been said.

Moderator: Gary, would you like react to that?

Habermas: I would love to react to that. In probably two minutes or less! No. Okay, Tony, notice you said Jesus was crucified, and then you said, "I think he died," or something like that. "I think but I'm not positive" or "I think, but let's just look at this," something like that?

Flew: No, that Pilate thought he was dead, but very early. You know, Pilate was surprised at a report of death, and he, after all, had in that rebellious Jewish part of the Empire the experience of crucifying other people.

Habermas: Yes, that was in Mark 15. Let me ask you a question: so you like Mark, right?

Flew: Yes.

Habermas: Tony, it's going to take me a little while to explain the detailed answers to your questions. So you say the Gospel of Mark is a good source, then. Well, let me make a few comments about crucifixion. We know a lot about crucifixion today and what happens on the cross, for several reasons. Unfortunately, some people have been crucified in recent history. Further, a number of medical doctors have actually asked for volunteers to be crucified. I know at least one of those medical doctors who asked for volunteers to come in and get up on a cross.

What they find out is this: you don't fake death by crucifixion. I know you're not saying that Jesus faked death. But you don't get down off the cross alive. You don't have to use nails, and it doesn't even have to be a typical cross. But if you're hanging long enough, here's what happens according to a majority of medical researchers: when you're hanging in this position, with your arms above your head, the weight of your body pulls down on the muscles surrounding your lungs—the intercostal, pectoral and deltoid muscles—and the muscles constrict your lungs. When the weight of your body pulls down on these muscles, while you are in the low position on the cross, your knees are bent and you're slumped down, then you begin asphyxiating. And you'll die fairly quickly if you don't do something about it.

In an experiment in Cologne, Germany, done by a medical doctor some years ago, the males who volunteered were simply tied to boards. That's all they did, and they lost consciousness in a maximum of twelve minutes. They lost consciousness and didn't have that much longer to live in that position. So when you hang on a cross, assuming your feet are tied or nailed, you push up into a position where you relieve those muscles around your lungs. But you can't stand there very long, especially if you're standing on nails.[2] You're fighting against gravity and you're pulling, and it is difficult to keep doing this. So you can basically stay alive as long as you can keep pushing up and down.

But when you can't push up anymore, you slump down in a low position, and that's when it's over relatively quickly. So all a centurion had to do when Jesus was on the cross was to be aware of the crucifixion and notice when the victim was standing up and when he was in the down position. When you are down for, let's say, thirty minutes, they're pretty much sure he's dead.

Now I invite you to check this out. Dozens of medical articles have been published on this process, one about fifteen years ago in the

---

[2]For a description, see Robert K. Wilcox, *Shroud* (New York: Macmillan, 1977), pp. 23-25, 161.

Journal of the American Medical Association [JAMA].[3] In that article, three scholars, including a pathologist from the Mayo Clinic, wrote Jesus' death certificate. They concluded that he died due to asphyxiation, complicated by shock and congestive heart failure. So that's one reason to know that Jesus died.

Second, it was common—and we have a number of references to this in ancient history—for a death blow to be delivered, the final coup de grâce, to somebody on a cross. We have a case where a person was threatened with a bow and arrow; we have a case where a fellow had his skull crushed before he died.[4] Breaking ankles is another way to ensure the victim's death. If the victim cannot push back up again, they asphyxiate. While they did not break Jesus' ankles, we're told that they stabbed him in the chest. We have other cases outside the New Testament where the crucified were stabbed.

We're told that blood and water came from the wound. The predominant medical explanation is that around the heart there is a sac, the pericardium, and it holds a watery fluid. So predominantly among these medical doctors, it is thought Jesus was stabbed in the heart, because that's the best explanation for the presence of the water—from the sac around the heart. So in that *JAMA* article, they concluded that Jesus was dead when the spear entered his body, but if he was not, the spear would have killed him.

Almost no scholar today questions Jesus' death by crucifixion. In fact, John Dominic Crossan—a cofounder of the Jesus Seminar—said the fact that Jesus died by crucifixion is as sure as any fact could ever be. Now, why would he say that? He mentions what is known about the process of crucifixion.[5]

But third, as the very liberal scholar David Strauss asserted 150 years ago, the chief problem with the swoon theory is logical in na-

[3]William D. Edwards, Wesley J. Gabel and Floyd E. Hosmer, "On the Physical Death of Jesus Christ," *Journal of the American Medical Association* 255 (March 1986), pp. 1455-63.
[4]Martin Hengel, *Crucifixion* (Philadelphia: Fortress, 1977), p. 70.
[5]John Dominic Crossan, *Jesus: A Revolutionary Biography* (San Francisco: Harper-SanFrancisco, 1994), pp. 145-58.

ture. If Jesus was weak and sickly and thought to be dead, but emerged from the tomb alive, then we have another sort of issue. So then he went and "appeared" to his disciples. But the problem is, they would see that he was alive, but they would never think he was *risen*. So picture how Jesus would inevitably look: sweating, hunched over, with his wounds opened up again. He hasn't even washed his hair; he's dripping blood so that there's a path behind him. The chief issue is that the disciples would never conclude that he was raised. They would only think he was alive, and that is a huge problem. To paraphrase Strauss, the disciples would get a doctor rather than proclaim Jesus to be risen.[6]

This is because Jesus would convince them that he was *alive*, but if there is no *risen* Jesus, then there is nothing on which to ground Christian teachings. If he is alive, that's great; but if they didn't believe he was actually raised from the dead, there would be no reason to accept the believer's resurrection. After all, as Paul and others would teach later, without the resurrection, there was no Christianity.

Could you imagine Peter over in the corner when Jesus struggled into the room? Peter might proclaim, "Oh boy, someday I'm going to have a resurrection body just like his." About twenty times in the New Testament, we are told that believers concluded that they will be raised like Jesus. The point is they couldn't believe that if they thought he was alive but not raised. So I'm sorry that I took so long on this explanation, but there are a few thoughts for you.[7] I didn't know if you wanted me to talk about the burial, too, but go ahead, you can respond.

Moderator: [To Flew] I don't know the extent to which your reser-

---

[6]David Strauss, *A New Life of Jesus*, 2nd ed. (Edinburgh: Williams and Norgate, 1879), 1:412. Albert Schweitzer stated that Strauss's critiques destroyed such naturalistic hypotheses, and he listed no one who preferred the swoon theory after 1840. See Albert Schweitzer, *The Quest of the Historical Jesus*, trans. W. Montgomery (New York: Macmillan, 1968), p. 56.

[7]For an in-depth discussion of Jesus' death by crucifixion, see Habermas, *The Historical Jesus*, pp. 69-75.

vations about the resurrection hang on your questions regarding Jesus' actual death, but if you want to say more about that, go ahead.

Habermas: Tony, you did say that you thought he died.

Flew: Well, yes, that's right. I still am puzzled about what evidence there is that there was an actual burial. Because, as you know, I believe the resurrection appearances were grief-related. I don't know if you want to call them visions or just experiences—for the existence of which there is apparently immensely strong evidence. No friend of ours has ever had one of these grief-related experiences, but apparently they are common. So that's the line I'm inclined to take, and these experiences would clearly be experiences of the dead person as they were when they were alive, so they wouldn't be experiences of a real person at all. But I would still like to know whether there was an actual burial.

Habermas: What do you think about any questions regarding his death? Are you satisfied on those? Do you think that what I've said is decent enough?

Flew: Yes, I should have thought so.

Habermas: Okay, good.

Flew: Yes, in view of the evidence about the effects of crucifixion, it suggests that this is a much quicker death than people have thought that it was.

Habermas: Just to clarify, people *could* be on a cross for days, and that's probably why Pilate asked that question. It depends on how long you can keep pushing up and down, but don't forget he was beaten severely, as well. So I think some extraordinary things were done in his case, and so that probably shortened it. He was on the cross for six hours. Well, should I address the burial?

Moderator: Go ahead.

Habermas: First of all, I'd say that whether or not he was buried doesn't always play a major role in resurrection discussions. If a person is truly dead, even if you have no idea where the body is, if you see him again afterward, now that's an issue.

But let's talk about Jesus' burial for a few moments.[8] Here are some of the data: it's reported in all four Gospels, in multiple sources. Everything we have says that he was buried in a tomb. Moreover, there are no early sources to the contrary. That twofold combination right there should be determinative if there are no other contrary reasons.

You also had religious leaders who were at the cross and who wanted Jesus to die. The Romans' job was to make sure of that outcome and to see the act to its completion, which included the burial. Further, Matthew, as well as two other writers, Justin Martyr[9] and Tertullian,[10] all report that, by blaming the disciples, the Jewish observers actually admitted that the place of burial was unoccupied. Now that would be a pretty incredible admission if no one was ever buried there in the first place.

If you want additional considerations, many critical scholars believe that the Gospel of Mark made use of a pre-Markan Passion narrative. Mark is already early, only about thirty-five years after the cross. Obviously, if this source is even earlier, that's rather significant. Additionally the choice of Joseph of Arimathea as the chief male who asked for Jesus' body [Mk 15:43-46] makes sense, since he is a very obscure figure in the early traditions.

I think that the best witness to Jesus' burial may well be the fact that, in all four Gospels, it was the women who were the first to discover on Sunday morning that the tomb no longer held Jesus' body. Although there were exceptions, in the Mediterranean world in general, female testimony was normally avoided wherever possible in courts of law, especially in crucial issues, and it was often disbelieved. My point is, if you're fabricating the account of the burial, then don't allow the case for the disappearance of the body to rely on female testimony. Obviously, that would invite ancient lis-

---

[8]For a list of reasons to believe Jesus was buried in a tomb, see Habermas, *The Historical Jesus*, pp. 126-29.
[9]*Dialogue with Trypho* 108.
[10]*On Spectacles* 30.

teners to reject the story from the outset.

So here are more than a half-dozen reasons for the historicity of Jesus' burial, and we could add others as well. But I think that's probably why virtually no scholars question that Jesus was buried. If he's dead, he's got to be buried somewhere, right? What do you think?

Flew: Yes.

Habermas: Yes, okay.

Flew: Yes, he does have to be buried somewhere, but not necessarily in the official tomb.

Habermas: But all those reasons I just provided are reasons for burial in the "official" tomb. In making a case in the ancient world, seven or eight arguments are a whole lot of reasons. This is not my view, but ultimately somebody could say, "I simply don't know what happened at the burial, but the real issue is whether Jesus was dead and alive." If you're dead, then you ought not be seen by people later. So that's the chief issue.

Flew: But, of course, the Jewish opposition was much concerned that this death should be final.

Habermas: I'm sure you're right. And the more they wanted to be sure he was dead, that's more reason to believe he was both dead and buried, because they would want to see the process through, right? They wouldn't just walk away and leave him hanging there. They'd want to make sure they see this thing to completion. That, by the way, is what we are told in the Gospel of Matthew.

Flew: Yes, I suppose it makes the most sense to say that the disciples refused to believe that Jesus was alive again simply in some odd sort of drastic continuation of the same old life, right? They wanted to finally end this distressing opposition by the religious leaders.

Habermas: Along that line, in your lecture this afternoon you mentioned that the book of Acts was a pretty good source. There is an enigmatic reference there, only half a verse long. We're not given any further explanation, but it says that the church was founded and Christianity spread, and a large number of Jewish priests came to faith [Acts 6:7]. That's just an incredible statement about the leaders whose group opposed the Christian message and who knew the original story. Why did they convert?

Flew: What was going on in Jerusalem at that time was very puzzling, wasn't it? Both the opposition as well as the counter-response. I mean, there was a very big conflict between the official view of the Jewish leaders and the Christians.

Habermas: That reminds me—the fact that all of this occurred in Jerusalem is one more reason to believe the "official" burial account. Let's say that a very popular and local holy man died and was buried just a half-mile from here. And let's add that many are now proclaiming that, just three days later, his grave is empty. We can go see it for ourselves. I imagine that whether we believe it or not, many of us would go, since it is such a short trip. But if it happened in Rome or Tokyo, I imagine most of us wouldn't go. But if the grave was located at the end of your street or a few blocks away, I imagine some would check out the reports. Similarly, Jerusalem is the last place to proclaim the death, burial and empty tomb of Jesus unless it could be confirmed. Right? Because many could have taken a Sunday-afternoon stroll and gotten there easily enough; it's the last place to preach. So the fact that the earliest message was proclaimed in this city is one more reason to think there were checks and balances in this town. People could tell if their proclamation was true, since the earliest preaching was in Jerusalem.

Flew: Yes, the whole scenario is Jerusalem; it is the crucial place, isn't it? Jesus' trip from the backwoods up to Jerusalem constitutes the crucial challenge to traditional authority. Entering the temple, of course, would provoke the traditional authorities, wouldn't it?

Habermas: Proclaiming the message later in Rome would also be a thorn in Rome's side, because as we read in Suetonius and others, Rome had emperor worship.

Flew: Yes.

Habermas: Remember Pilate's question to Jesus?

Flew: Yes.

Habermas: "Are you the King of the Jews?"[Mk 15:2]. I don't think Jesus was any kind of a threat to the Roman regime, but they may have disagreed—with the large crowds at Passover.

Flew: Almost certainly, because the Jewish people were a major threat to the Roman imperial regime. And they were much more numerous actually than is generally believed, because of the very large number of Jews who had moved into other parts of the Empire, outside the area of modern Israel. They were a large group, exceptionally well educated and, perhaps from the point of view of the emperor, an exceptionally troublesome group.

Habermas: At Passover, they would return to Jerusalem, so this is already a rough time of the year for the Roman soldiers.

Flew: And the Romans had already had one or two, and were soon to have another, major conflict with the Jews.

Habermas: In A.D. 66.

Flew: Quite, yes.

ASSESSING THE CLAIMS OF THE RESURRECTION

Moderator: [To Flew] Well, you have some qualms, but it sounds to me like—and correct me if I'm wrong—but it sounds to me as if you're virtually conceding that perhaps you see our list of facts as relatively uncontroversial. So my best guess is that you think there's a better explanation for these data, if they are facts, than the actual resurrection. So I'm wondering if you could say something about that.

Flew: Well, surely the actual belief in the resurrection entails more than just the belief that Jesus was resurrected. It's what's supposed to have happened later: Jesus acquiring a status as somehow more than a chap who has been so fortunate as to be resurrected, of whom there are other biblical examples, aren't there? Lazarus, for instance, is supposed to have been raised, after a longer period of death than Jesus, actually; and there are at least a couple of other accounts in the Old Testament, one in 1 Kings and one in 2 Kings. And

I believe there may be some similar accounts elsewhere in the Bible, but there are all these, and clearly they don't comprise the established essentials of the Christian religion anything like the whole story about Jesus' resurrection does. Of course, the nature of being resurrected in Jesus' case makes this more exciting than any of the others, due, to put it mildly, to the charismatic character of Jesus. After my recent comparisons with the prophet of Islam, the resurrection of Jesus, in view of his life and sayings and so on, is clearly going to be of more world historical interest than the resurrection of Lazarus. It's the "something more" that I am altogether unclear about.

Habermas: Especially if, as Christians believe, Lazarus had to die again and Jesus didn't have to do so, obviously making all the difference in the world.

Flew: Yes, it clearly does, yes.

Habermas: Especially given Jesus' claims.

Flew: Exactly so, yes.

Habermas: Humanly speaking, anyone can make extraordinary claims. But if Jesus made claims that truly were *extraordinary*—perhaps even without real parallels in the history of religions—and then if he's raised from the dead, well, that's really significant. After all, dead people don't do much, so if he's dead, he is not going to be raising himself.

Flew: Right.

Habermas: So, if he has made extraordinary claims, and if, as he claimed, he is acted upon by Another who raised him from the dead, now people are asking, and I think justly, "Whoa! Who is this guy supposed to be?" Because in the New Testament, the resurrection provides the evidence for the claims, hence its centrality, which is one of the historical facts that we started with tonight. Obviously you don't believe in the resurrection, so what do you think is a better explanation of the data?

Flew: Well, I'm wanting to know what is the something more, other than the character of Jesus himself, which makes this of special significance? I mean, surely he is supposed to go to another place, isn't he?

Habermas: I think the best evidence we have for the resurrection is the apostle Paul and, no matter how skeptical you get, even people like Michael Martin and G. A. Wells concede that Paul was an eyewitness to what he believed was a resurrection appearance of Jesus—another of the facts up there on the screen. The same goes for James, the brother of Jesus. He was also an unbeliever during Jesus' life. That's conceded by virtually all scholars. These two men, James, the brother of Jesus, and Paul, were unbelievers until they were convinced they met the risen Jesus. Now we have Paul's testimony firsthand, and that's what makes him such a powerful witness.

Flew: Yes.

Habermas: It's rare to find any New Testament scholars who deny a Pauline authorship for 1 Corinthians. Paul states a couple of times that he saw the resurrected Jesus. In 9:1 he asks, "Am I not an apostle; have I not seen the Lord?"[11] Then in 15:3 and following, he passes on data that he received from someone else. He says, "I gave you as of first importance what I also received, how that Christ died for our sins according to the scriptures, and that he was buried, and that he rose again the third day according to the scripture, and appeared," and then he lists appearances to both individuals and groups. Then Paul added, "Last of all he appeared to me." Then he concludes just three verses later, "Whether it is I or the other apostles, this is what we preach." So not only is Paul giving us his own experience, he's our best window on the other apostles and what they were preaching regarding Jesus' resurrection.

In Galatians 1 and 2—another undoubtedly Pauline book—twice and perhaps even three times Paul made trips up to Jerusalem. He met with all three of the best-known Christians of that time: Peter, John and James, the brother of Jesus, who were believers before Paul.

---

[11]This and all Scripture quotations during the debate are paraphrases.

He said that he set his gospel message before them so they could check it out [Gal 2:2]. They agreed with him; they didn't add anything at all to his message [2:6]. I mean this respectfully, but today we would call Paul obsessive because he went to Jerusalem, and that's not just like getting on a plane and making an hour plane flight. That's a pretty good trip. He went up there once in Galatians 1, then a second time in Galatians 2, and he may have gone a third time, depending on what we do with Acts 15. So he made two or three trips up to Jerusalem specifically to talk to the main disciples to ascertain this gospel message, and he reported the conclusion that they were preaching the same thing he was. So, what do you get from this? The earliest apostles were all totally convinced that they saw the risen Jesus. How can we explain that data better?

Flew: But are they repeating, substantially, the things that were said earlier about or by Jesus, or are they uttering a new message?

Habermas: I'm not sure what you're asking.

Flew: Well, roughly they are repeating his claims, aren't they?

Habermas: They're repeating their beliefs that the gospel message was true, including that they saw him.

Flew: Yes, yes.

Habermas: And so we have their testimony from a very early date. In fact, most critical scholars think we can date Paul's reception of this testimony to A.D. 35, which is only five years after the cross. This isn't the date of the events themselves, but his trip to Jerusalem, where he received this testimony.

You could even work it out: if you put the cross at 30, Paul's conversion is usually placed at one or two years later, so let's just say two—that's 32. Paul explains in Galatians 1 that three years later he went up to Jerusalem to talk to the other apostles. So two plus three equals five, or approximately A.D. 35. So Paul gives us the year markers right there in his works. The German historian Hans von Campenhausen states that these Pauline texts, 1 Corinthians 15 and Galatians 1 and 2, give us all the checks and balances we would want from an ancient historical text.[12]

Flew: Oh, yes.

Habermas: In ancient history, we often have gaps of a century or more before.

Flew: Oh, yes.

Habermas: Here we get something from five years afterward, and then of course that's just when Paul received it from the other disciples. They knew it before he did, so there's no gap at all, you know, if he got this five years later. Actually, he's kind of late; as he said, "I was born out of due time." The other apostles were Christians before him. So there's virtually no gap there at all. He got it five years later. They knew it before he did.

Flew: Yes, Paul had a similar vision, but surely there's supposed to be something extra, isn't there, about the future of Jesus? We have a resurrected Jesus of whom people are having visions and so forth and so on, and then he is supposed to be going somewhere, isn't he?

Moderator: What troubles you about that?

Flew: Well, he's not going to be a continual resident of the planet Earth, is he?

Habermas: Why should that be an issue? If he was raised, he can go anywhere he wants, can't he? Why would going back to heaven, however he got there, be an issue for someone who was raised from the dead? I would think the much bigger miracle would be the resurrection, right? Let's put it this way: if Jesus Christ is who he claimed to be, and he was raised to demonstrate it, I wouldn't stand in his way wherever he wanted to go.

Flew: No, but he's claiming to be the Son of God.

Habermas: Right.

Flew: Now that seems to be a rather odd claim. This isn't so obvious to me, now, this claim of having a special relationship to the ruler of the universe.

---

[12]Hans von Campenhausen, "The Events of Easter and the Empty Tomb," in *Tradition and Life in the Church* (Philadelphia: Fortress, 1968), p. 44.

Habermas: Yes, he claimed it was a unique relationship too. He said he was the only one who has this.

Flew: Well, yes, I can see why that should be claimed to be unique, but it's not clear to me what it's supposed to involve, really. I mean, we have the development of the doctrine of the Trinity, which is a difficult belief, to put it mildly.

Habermas: What would you do with a person who claimed to be the Son of God, who claimed to have a unique relationship with the God of the universe? He made some other pretty interesting claims too. He claimed to forgive sin, and the leaders responded, "Hey, you can't do that; that's blasphemy." But Jesus retorted, "Well, to show you I can do it, I'll heal this man." Here he also claims to be the Son of Man, which, contrary to popular opinion, is not a human claim. In first-century Jewish literature, "Son of Man" is a very lofty claim. In fact, it probably contributed eventually to his death. So Jesus makes these claims about himself, including uniqueness with the God of the universe, and they say, "Well, how do we know this?" And he responds, "Well, because I'm going to rise from the dead," and then he does it. Do you listen to him at that point? Do you think, "Uh oh, this is getting too close for comfort"?

Flew: Well, it suddenly gets too close for comfort, yes. But it remains a very perplexing claim.

Habermas: But the resurrection sort of puts his money where his mouth is, you know what I mean?

Flew: Oh, yes.

Habermas: It's one thing to make a claim, but then to be raised is rather special.

Flew: Yes.

Habermas: First of all, we don't even have claims like that from the founders of the major world religions.

Flew: Certainly not.

Habermas: So even the claim is rather extraordinary. That doesn't make it true; it just makes it extraordinary.

Flew: Absolutely.

Habermas: And we don't have claims from the orthodox followers of other major religious founders that their man was raised. So altogether, it is extraordinary.

Flew: In the case of Islam, we don't have claims to any miracles at all, and the point that Aquinas was trying to make in the *Summa Contra Gentiles* was precisely that there are no miracles even claimed regarding those founders. Are there any others?

Habermas: Well, I think at least with the major founders. Edwin Yamauchi, professor of ancient history at the University of Miami of Ohio, stated that no other founder of a major world religion has miracles reported of him in the early, primary documents.[13]

Flew: I think that's right, yes.

Habermas: Now again, these are the claims, and then Jesus places everything on the resurrection. That's the big event. That's why Christians are excited about this.

Flew: Yes.

CONSIDERING THE RESURRECTION APPEARANCES

Moderator: Professor Flew, you seem to have shifted a bit here. Is your issue that the resurrection never took place or that the resurrection leads one to make fantastic claims about what it means to be the Son of God? Is it those sorts of claims or is it the resurrection per se, that there's a better explanation for it as a hallucination or something like this?

Flew: Well, I am intensely puzzled by the whole situation here. Even if you grant that the resurrection has occurred, this seems to me to be an event so extraordinary that I don't know what's to be said about it at all. And I don't believe in the objectivity of the appearances. I can see that we have a claim that the body was resurrected, but the claim to the resurrection seems to me based on the appearances.

---

[13]Edwin Yamauchi, *Jesus, Zoroaster, Buddha, Socrates, Muhammad*, rev. ed. (Downers Grove, Ill.: InterVarsity Press, 1972), p. 40.

Habermas: That's fair.

Flew: And I don't think those appearances are an adequate basis for it. In all this, I think one ought to notice that any experiences of claims to what is nowadays called the paranormal—what used to be investigated by what was called psychical research—any claims to the genuineness of such occurrences have to be founded, if they're to be believed, on an extraordinary amount of evidence. Anything that is conceived to be miraculous falls into this category, because one must approach any question about an alleged miracle with a pretty stubborn presumption that it didn't really happen, because its extraordinariness depends on its being a unique event.

Habermas: Okay, so what would you say? We have these historical facts, which are quite extraordinary data.

Flew: Yes.

Habermas: What could we propose in place of the resurrection?

Flew: Well, it's the continuous activity of Christ that is supposedly supported by the appearances.

Habermas: But if he's appearing, if he is genuinely appearing after being dead . . .

Flew: But that's what I don't think was the case. We have a whole lot of people who think they saw him, but then this is what happens with . . .

Habermas: What is a better explanation of the historical data we have?

Flew: That they were grief-related appearances.

Habermas: Now you don't mean *real* appearances?

Flew: Oh yes, well, okay, ostensible appearances. Yes, what seemed to them to be appearances—what the old-time philosophers would call sense data.

Habermas: Okay, so basically if you're going to say grief visions, you're saying hallucinations.

Flew: If you'd like, yes.

Habermas: Because the other way, it sounds like you were almost talking about a resurrection, and I know that's not what you're saying.

Moderator: That would have been a very short discussion if it were, wouldn't it?

Habermas: Right here on your campus, Tony Flew said that he likes the resurrection! No, okay, could these have been grief-related hallucinations? That's what Tony means when he says grief visions. We've discussed this a few times. A few years ago, we spent an entire discussion on grief visions—parts of three hours on this subject.[14]

Regarding any kind of hallucination hypothesis, whether grief-related or any other variety, probably no natural thesis is plagued by more difficulties.[15] Just quickly, here are a few of the problems: groups of people don't see the same hallucinations. Hallucinations are no more objective than dreams. By definition, the individual produces the mental image. Obviously I don't share the personal images you create.

Hallucinations are more radical than is sometimes thought too. When you misperceive something and take it to be what it is not, that is different. Hallucinations have no objective, external referent. It's like talking to my deceased grandmother, whom I just know all of you see right here beside me, when nothing objective corresponds to it. That's pretty radical as well as being a private claim. So any time we have groups of people who believe they saw the risen Jesus, they cannot share the same hallucination. That's highly problematic.

For example, we have discussed the pre-Pauline list of appearances in 1 Corinthians 15. There's hardly a critic around who will deny the early date of this list. Several appearances are to individuals: Peter, James and later Paul. But three groups are also listed: appearances to the Twelve, to all the apostles and to five hundred persons at once.

---

[14]See Habermas and Flew, *Resurrected?*, pp. 7-11.

[15]For details along with nineteen objections to various forms of the hallucination theory, including "grief visions," see Gary R. Habermas, "Explaining Away Jesus' Resurrection: The Recent Revival of Hallucination Theories," *Christian Research Journal* 23 (2001): 26-31, 47-49.

Group appearances are very difficult for hallucinations, because we don't hallucinate the same thing together. Another huge issue is the different personalities involved. You've got men and women who are indoors or outdoors, walking, standing or sitting. Changing scenarios also militate against hallucinations.

Further, the disciples weren't in the best frame of mind. One of the historical facts we posted earlier is that they were disillusioned; they were in a state of despair. Non-drug-induced hallucinations generally come from heightened states of awareness.

Another huge problem is the empty tomb. If they had hallucinated, there still would have been a body there. But in Jerusalem, you could have strolled down to the tomb and saw that it was empty, but not if hallucinations are the best explanation.

One more thing might be said, though we could list others. Hallucinations generally don't change lives. The more common cause is bodily deprivation, such as lack of food or water. In the case of Navy Seals research, these soldiers are talked out of these hallucinations by their friends. One reported that an octopus was waving at him and smiling; another picked up an oar and started swinging it at the porpoises jumping overhead. One soldier jumped into the water because he thought that a train was coming straight for them. Now, these experiences obviously aren't objective. Later when the soldiers were interviewed regarding the porpoises or the train or the octopus, they reported two chief reasons why they no longer believed this: those things don't happen, and their buddies didn't see them.

Now apply those same two reasons to the resurrection appearances: my buddies didn't see it (in the case of individual hallucinations), and these things don't happen (dead men don't rise, to cite David Hume). So they talked themselves out of it?

Anyway, there are many other problems too. James and Paul are two huge issues, because they were unbelievers, thus highly unlikely to manufacture hallucinations.

Moderator: [To Habermas] Can I just ask a question: is the issue, then, that we are comparing improbabilities? It would be wildly improbable to have a group hallucination of this sort, but I wonder what the improbability of that is, compared to the improbability of someone being dead rising again and actually being the Son of God? It seems to me that the intrinsic improbability is greater on the latter than the former, isn't it?

Habermas: Do you know you're citing the fellow seated right there [points to Flew]?

Moderator: I told you he was an eminent philosopher!

Habermas: Yes, that's right. He wrote the article on "miracles" for the *Encyclopedia of Philosophy*, where he raised that same issue.[16] It's a great question. But to me the problem is this: Okay, what's more unlikely? A group hallucination or a resurrection? And one might think, on the surface, that a resurrection would be stranger than a group hallucination, even though we don't know of any documented group hallucinations in history either. Still, a resurrection seems stranger.

The chief problem here is that the hallucinations are not one-time exceptions. If our reports are true, there are appearances to unbelievers, as well as group appearances to the five hundred at once, to all the apostles, to the disciples and to the women. So you have several groups. Now I would ask you, what's more likely? A number of unique group hallucinations, or a single resurrection? It's not just one group appearance. I agree with you, it is a probabilities issue.

Moderator: Right, well, I don't know that you have to be committed to . . . Some people say they have an appearance, and they don't.

Flew: And the vision to the five hundred—we really don't have evidence of that which would satisfy anyone if it wasn't accompanied by things that they were more inclined to believe, like the appearances to Paul and so on. I mean, that claim is tossed out like, "Oh, yes, and there was an appearance to five hundred." That's always

---

[16]*Encyclopedia of Philosophy*, s.v. "miracles," Antony Flew, pp. 350, 352.

seemed to me a very odd, arbitrary and implausible addition to the whole thing.

Habermas: The reason it's taken seriously is that it's in the pre-Pauline list in 1 Corinthians 15. He said he received it from somebody else and critics think it can be dated to A.D. 35 in Jerusalem, so this list is taken very seriously.

By the way, this particular portion itself is a creedal text—including non-Pauline terms, a codified list, the immediate syntax before and after, and so on. There are dozens of these creeds in the New Testament. They're texts that were oral testimony dating before the earliest New Testament book was written. Paul says he received this, and again, most critical scholars place this reception in Jerusalem about A.D. 35. The reason scholars take the appearance of the five hundred so seriously is that it appears in the list that Paul presents in 1 Corinthians 15—because it comes from the earliest strand of evidence.

Flew: I'm afraid that this thing tends to discredit anything it is associated with, it seems to me.

Habermas: Why would it be an issue? I mean, if Jesus preached to larger groups than that—we have the famous feeding of the five thousand incident, there's another group of four thousand—if there were thousands of people on occasion, why is it a priori odd that five hundred people would be together this time?

Flew: Well, I'm afraid that the feeding of the five thousand is one of the statements that I find great difficulty in believing.

Habermas: What I'm saying is, as far as a group of people coming together, five hundred is no problem, say, in the Passover season. But the issue is not how many people . . .

Flew: But the group of five hundred having a vision is much more remarkable than a group of 500 or 501 or 499 . . .

Moderator: Eating fish.

Flew: . . . coming together. It seems to me that it is utterly disproportionate to all the other claims and would require very much stronger evidence.

Habermas: What do you think about Jesus appearing to twelve people at once? Or appearing to the apostles? Are you comfortable with that?

Flew: Ummm . . .

Habermas: You see, if he appeared to anybody, you still have a resurrection.

WHAT COUNTS AS EVIDENCE?

Moderator: [To Flew] May I ask you this question? You don't like the appearances, but what would count for a resurrection? Could anything count, or is that in principle just so wildly implausible that nothing would count? Perhaps video would? I don't know.

Flew: Well, yes.

Moderator: That would help.

Habermas: I just happen to have some photos here. They'll be on sale afterward.

Flew: A special bargain offer.

Habermas: Just tonight. But that's a good question, Joe. What counts as great evidence?

Flew: I'm not sure I can answer that one at all, no.

Habermas: Let me ask this way: how about your essay "Theology and Falsification"?[17]

Flew: Yes.

Habermas: An article that you wrote in 1955.

Flew: It was published in 1955, I think, yes.

Habermas: Well, it was good. You said it counts against a view when it is unfalsifiable.

Flew: Absolutely.

Habermas: Is your present view unfalsifiable?

Flew: My unbelief, you mean?

Habermas: Your unbelief specifically in the resurrection.

---

[17]Antony Flew, "Theology and Falsification," in *New Essays in Philosophical Theology*, ed. Antony Flew and Alasdair MacIntyre (London: SCM Press, 1955), pp. 96-99.

Flew: Yes.

Habermas: If we have our list of historical facts and every time you bring up a natural possibility, each one seems to be opposed by a number of rejoinders, at what point do you say that it begins to look like a real resurrection? Or conversely, at what point would you say that your view is or is not falsifiable?

Flew: I think the only honest answer is that I don't know. I am not sure.

Habermas: You know Tony Flew is responding to Tony Flew here.

Flew: Yes, yes, I think the unfalsifiability of *unbelief* is somehow a different problem from the unfalsifiability of a *belief.*

Habermas: But if you can't falsify your own view, and if there is no probable rejoinder to the resurrection, and you're left with, "Well, I don't want to believe it anyway," of course that's your right.

Flew: Yes.

Habermas: So it's your belief that your position on the resurrection is unfalsifiable. Right?

Flew: Yes, but I suppose one could always imagine things that would be just overwhelming confirmation.

Habermas: Would a resurrection falsify your belief? Could this be it? Could this be the data that would do it? I mean, in principle, the resurrection would falsify it, wouldn't it?

Flew: Yes, I suppose I have an almost invincible disinclination to believe the whole resurrection story, yes, because it seems to me so wildly inconsistent with everything else that happens in the universe.

Habermas: Maybe the universe is different too. That's another issue, but perhaps . . .

Flew: Yes.

Habermas: . . . this might be one of those singularities, as you might say, that should make you question a lot of other items of your system.

Flew: Oh yes, I think the answer to that must be certainly yes. Yes, that it is just so extraordinary if actually the whole thing happens, you know. Straightforwardly, it is a creature of flesh and blood that the apostles see, and so on.

Habermas: It would be rather wonderful, wouldn't it?

Flew: And that Thomas could touch him with his thumb, or was it his finger, and all that. The whole total story is so wildly unlike the things that happen in Los Angeles even!

Habermas: Earlier I lectured on the topic of near-death experiences. An NDE is not a resurrection, to be sure. But take a highly evidenced NDE where someone recalls data during an EEG that is flat for three hours, and they report things they saw during that time, although their brain apparently wasn't working. These experiences raise the bar a little. NDEs say, "Wow, this world might be different from what we think it is."

Flew: Yes, this is going to be looked at. It has been studied by people as the putative phenomena of extrasensory perception and, of course, there are complications in the theory that there is retroactive sensory perception.

Habermas: But even so, you have something special here. What if we gave a definition of life after death as something like extrasensory perception after death? What I mean is, this notion of extrasensory perception may delay the conclusion, but if you have people reporting things when their brain isn't functioning, and they seem to be alive and well, and we have dozens of these highly evidenced cases . . .

Flew: But they're extrasensorially perceiving things that were going on when they were brain-dead, isn't that it?

Habermas: Brain-dead, that's right. I'm not trying to get us off the subject. I'm just saying there could be things in this world that show the world isn't what we thought.

Flew: Oh, very much so.

Habermas: That's all I was saying.

Moderator: [To Habermas] Could I ask you a question about that? Because that sort of thing would say to me that, if the world—and by the world you mean the laws of nature—may be different from what we understand it to be, do you really want to say that the Christian confidence in the resurrection is a part of the natural order of things that we just haven't discovered yet, or do you want to say it is a supernatural intervention?

Habermas: Jesus states these special things about himself, claiming he'll be raised from the dead to show who he was. Basically, he says, "I'm the only one who knows the God of the universe, and the resurrection will show that he's raised me from the dead to confirm this." When you put that together, that's where you get the supernatural conclusion, due to his claim that the God of the universe is acting upon him. I mean, that is a supernatural connection.

On the other point—the natural plane—if somebody said to me, "Well, what if we find an explanation in the future? What if, a hundred years from now, we find something that makes sense?" I would just say the same thing we say about all scientific theses: "Well, then, let's face it in a hundred years. As far as we're concerned, we need to decide on the data we have. We can only deal with what we have right now." I think that's something about which we can agree. You can only make a present decision based on what you have presently. So to answer your question directly, Jesus made these special claims, and the resurrection showed that the God of the universe was acting upon him. So I would say this is supernatural.

Moderator: Well, it just occurs to me that if it were more like the extrasensory thing—that, surely, someone could have the ability and be mistaken even about what the nature of that ability was. I once heard a lecture where someone claimed that Jesus' death on the cross was not real, but that it was a technique that he learned while studying yoga. I took yoga for a year, and I didn't get that "surviving the crucifixion" lesson. I think I missed that day.

But I'm wondering what would warrant the inference that, just because he makes a claim, there's this uniqueness. You're making the case that there is strong historical evidence that the appearances are real, and he makes an additional claim that there is a God and that "I'm the Son of God." But I'm just having a hard time making that compatible with the view that maybe the world is different from what we know. Because the world being different would make it part of natural phenomena that we just don't know yet. And it seems to me that the Christian view would be something else; what would it be to have a whole bunch of *natural* evidence that somehow adds up to *super*natural?

Habermas: If you are referring to NDE research, I don't think the realm of the afterlife is a natural realm. Further, the afterlife is part of the same realm as inhabited by the resurrection. So by raising the evidence for NDEs, I am decidedly not moving from the natural to the supernatural sphere, but providing evidence for *another* example of the supernatural, and in the same general area as well. This should prevent the common claim that the resurrection introduces a concept for which there are absolutely no comparisons.

The resurrection itself would be pretty tough to explain naturally. David Hume says that it would be a miracle if a man returned from the dead.[18] So we're not adding a bunch of "nonsupernaturals" to get a "supernatural." The resurrection *itself* would seem to be a very supernatural claim, beyond any laws of nature. I know you were teasing about the yoga training, but if anyone is held under water for ten minutes, then they're dead, whether they are practicing yoga or not. And a person on the cross, if what I said earlier is true, is also dead.

Moderator: I have no doubts about that.

Habermas: By the way, I know a pathologist who got up very briefly onto a model cross. He told me that, after only two minutes, he experienced excruciating pain in his chest. If a person is going to hang in that low position on the cross without pushing up, no disci-

---

[18]Also in R. Douglas Geivett and Gary R. Habermas, eds., *In Defense of Miracles* (Downers Grove, Ill.: InterVarsity Press, 1997), pt. 1.

pline is going to keep them breathing. Those are the built-in checks and balances of crucifixion. I know you're not questioning that. When you mentioned yoga, I just repeated this. But there are built-in checks and balances on the cross that guarantee death.

IS BELIEF JUSTIFIABLE?

Moderator: Well, Professor Flew, according to your position, the best explanation for that data, if you're willing to accept it, is some kind of illusion. So, what is your response to the unlikelihood of a collective event? I know you're not a collectivist, but this would be a collectivist interpretation.

Flew: Back to the situation. I am going to say that I have almost an invincible unbelief. This is so unlike anything in the rest of my experience of the world that I just don't know how to cope with this at all.

Habermas: Is this "invincible unbelief" unfalsifiable?

Moderator: His view would be that if it's not falsifiable, it's meaningless.

Flew: No, no, I don't think this would be so. I suppose I can imagine a series of developments which would make it clear to me that the universe wasn't at all as I previously thought it to be. But, of course, I don't think anyone believes that this is going to happen. They believe that this is a unique, central position, you know. It is my position that any Christian believer would have to say about these facts or alleged facts that they are the most important facts in human history. They just don't have any analogy in any experience of anything else. This is essentially a once-for-all divine intervention in the affairs of the universe. Is that not roughly what the claim is?

Habermas: It would be a pretty major claim.

Flew: Yes.

Moderator: So it's your view that those who believe now in the resurrection—at least that their beliefs are not warranted; they're not justified?

Flew: No, I don't think I want to say with absolute confidence that they're not justified, because reasonable people may make disastrous mistakes on what they themselves have good reason to believe.

Moderator: So this is a disastrous mistake, but a rational one?

Flew: No, I don't want to say it is irrational for other people to believe in this. It seems to me it would be perfectly rational for *them* to believe in this, but *I* can't cope with this idea at all. It seems to me so unlike anything else that happens in the universe.

The way I would normally approach this is by taking a favorite example of mine. The commander of a unit of tanks who, because of the available intelligence that he had—and he had every reason to expect they had gotten it right (because they usually did so)—in fact leads his unit into a trap which massacres the lot of them. You cannot say that he was an irrational man being in that position. I think this idea can be extended to many other things—to some of the most recent arguments for the existence of God, for example. I think that people who already believe in God are quite rational in thinking this is a confirmation; ditto with the big bang theory.

If the main purpose of God in creating the whole universe was to have human beings, as it would appear from the book of Genesis, in which God is not apparently sustaining but only an initiating force, and therefore his creatures are reasonably free human beings—if his purpose were that, he would surely have created the universe as all the scientists of the Middle Ages believed he had—*as the center of the universe.* It's the view that was overthrown by the scientific work of Copernicus. But the idea that the creator of the universe would plan the universe so the eventual emergence of Earth and human beings was the product of an *extraordinarily* unlikely coincidence of the physical constants, all of which he presumably formed as the creator of the universe, it seems to me it's positively preposterous to think of this as a good reason for unbelievers to believe that God created the universe. But I think it's reasonable enough for the people who believe that already. This is confirmation. You show that he planned it all in this extremely subtle way and he made all the physical constants combine in this way so that it would happen like that.

Habermas: It would be wonderful, wouldn't it?

Flew: It would have been wonderful.

Habermas: That's the point.

Flew: I think it is an important thing to see that in these matters people can fundamentally disagree, though they are equally rational people. They're doing what it is entirely reasonable to think on the basis of what they already believe.

Habermas: Let me ask you a question about your tank illustration. Regarding a person who makes a rational but very wrong decision, if that was meant to be a parable of Christianity, it seems to me that the problem is that the knife cuts both ways, right? I mean atheism could be the tank commander too, right?

Flew: Oh yes, certainly.

Habermas: Okay.

Flew: I'm not saying that this is something that is reasonable for Christians but not for other people.

Habermas: So we're back to deciding on the data in front of us.

Flew: Yes, in the light of our own, as we think, most reasonable beliefs before we came to this problem.

Moderator: So if one already believes in a transcendent God, then belief in the resurrection can be rational? But if you don't . . .

Flew: I think this would be the case. I've only thought about it in light of the latest arguments for the existence of God, which were introduced before I started thinking about them. I was an adolescent before the big bang theory was formulated. How old can you get?

Moderator: I'm looking at a cheat sheet, and it says that it's almost time for closing statements from the speakers, after which we can have a period of questions and, with any luck, answers. So [to Flew], would you like to make a closing statement?

Flew: No, I have already said what I particularly wanted to say.

Habermas: That was the apex of your case.

Moderator: [To Habermas] Would you like to make a closing statement?

Habermas: Sure. When I leave tonight, I will remember the tank commander. Well, let me state a little bit about my methodology, which I haven't gotten to yet. I hope this will provide a context for everything I've said here. The method I use when speaking about the resurrection is not to assume that the Bible is inspired, or even reliable. I would rather work from a lowest common denominator and work up from there. We started tonight with a list of historical facts, and I think that's the best way to go. Tony and I basically agreed on these. In an earlier debate, we had almost total agreement. So Tony and I pretty much share this same foundation, and it's pretty much shared by the entire scholarly community, Christian and non-Christian alike. By beginning with such a basis, you don't have to object to something solely because it's found in the Bible, should you reject that source; this last response misses the point. The chief issue, then, is whether these are historical facts that are known on their own grounds, no matter what your position. So, do we have good reasons to accept them as historical?

I will mention that we have a dozen and a half non-Christian sources for Jesus outside the New Testament as well. Contrary to popular belief, Jesus is one of the most mentioned people in ancient history. In fact, the earliest comment about Jesus could well be from a Greek historian, predating the New Testament. And what he records, by the way, is a miracle. So tonight, I'm not proposing believing something because it's in the New Testament. I'm arguing that if all we know about the New Testament is that it's a book of ancient literature, and I'll just note that it was Dr. Flew who said in his lecture this afternoon that the New Testament comes with very good credentials, that's enough. I don't have to even make his assumption, since I can reach my conclusions with just the data like the list that we started with tonight—we must account for the facts.

Now, I was quite pleased to hear Tony say that Christians are rational in believing in the resurrection, given their belief structure. But I think you can get there another way too: the single historical fact that is the most crucial on our list is that the disciples believed that they saw the risen Jesus. They thought they saw the risen Jesus. Scholars say almost unanimously, "Well, of course they thought they saw the risen Jesus."

But did they *really* see him alive? Here's where you bring in all the other accompanying reasons—their transformed lives, they are willing to die for it, how do you account for James, and then Paul, who were both unbelievers? They also believed that Jesus appeared to them. So you have this belief that they thought Jesus appeared to them, and you ask, "Can I explain these facts with other natural hypotheses, given what I know of science or history or philosophy or anything?" And if the data still look as if Jesus appeared, then I think we have a problem if we're going to reject it, or if we say that my belief structure doesn't work here. You still have to deal with the data— it's your own data!

I will say, too, that I spent ten years searching. I used to argue with Christians and told them some pretty nasty things. I almost became a Buddhist. I ended up doing my doctoral dissertation on the resurrection and being convinced it happened. But then in 1995, I had a chance to test all of this firsthand. My wife passed away with stomach cancer. Actually, Tony knew her because he came to our home and stayed with us at the school for a couple of weeks.

And then of course you have all these issues about evil and pain. When all of this happened, a graduate student called me and asked, "Where would you be today if it weren't for the resurrection of Jesus?" And I realized that if Jesus was raised from the dead, it makes all the difference in the world. That meant my wife would be raised just like Jesus. That's pretty significant when I'm sitting there looking death in the face and watching her die.

I'll just end with the last verses of 1 Corinthians 15, the same passage we've been talking about tonight. Paul basically taunts death. At the end of the chapter, he says, "Death, where is your sting; grave, where is your victory?" He is basically saying, "You've got nothing, you've got nothing," because as he goes on to say, the answer is the resurrection of Jesus. Paul was a scholar. Earlier today Tony called him a very worthy philosopher, and Paul converted to Christianity because he saw the risen Jesus. So I'll end with that thought. For me, within my noetic structure, if the resurrection happened about A.D. 30, then it's an event that has continuing meaning today, for my family and all we went through in 1995. If you have the resurrection, you have plenty.

QUESTIONS FROM THE AUDIENCE

Moderator: So that concludes the official part of the conversation, and now it's your turn, if you like, to come to a microphone and ask a question. If you want to come up, make sure it is a question that you have and not a speech, and that the question is brief.

Habermas: Are they going to address it to one of us?

Moderator: And please address the question specifically to one or the other, and I see we have someone here, so go right ahead.

Question 1: Actually, I was hoping to hear from both of you, and I had two really quick ones. One is, what do both of you have to say about the speculation that the followers of Jesus moved the body of Jesus and hid it in order to keep the movement going? And the other is, does Jesus' divinity depend on the resurrection? If you have no resurrection, do you have no divinity? Are they dependent? Those are my questions.

Habermas: Okay, we have a couple of questions, so here's a couple of responses. The first question: what about the hypothesis that the disciples may have stolen the body to perpetrate their claim? In the history of responses to the resurrection, this one has hardly ever been held by any major critical scholars since Hermann Reimarus, a German rationalist, did it about 1760. If critics don't hold a theory, you can know that there are reasons why they don't, and there's a lot of problems with this one.

When somebody is willing to die for their position, no matter what it is—it could be an atheist dying for communism—you don't say they perpetrated a fraud. Let's say that they went ahead and died. You'd say, "I may not believe what they do, but it's clear that this person must have really believed what they taught."

Now, Tony will quickly point out that believing something doesn't make it true, and that's correct. But here's the point: if the disciples were willing to die for what they believed, and we have ample evidence of that—we can talk about it if you want, from early history—then they at least believed it. So to say they stole the body and then lied about the appearances seems to be a huge problem, for it is almost impossible to account for their actions. Plus you've got James and Paul, who were unbelievers. How do you get James and Paul involved in this plot? There's a lot of other issues too.

The other question was, can we have the deity of Jesus Christ without a resurrection? Theoretically, Jesus could have said, "I'm deity, take it or leave it." Or "I'm deity and I'll heal this person's leg to show it." Then you'll have to evaluate that on its own grounds and see what you think. So, yes, that could work, but what I'm saying is that the evidential value would be a lot lower, and further, that's not all Jesus claimed. Jesus said "I'm deity and I'll show it by being raised from the dead," so now he's making the ultimate claim. It's a stand or fall kind of view. That's why Paul says, if Christ has been raised, you know the Christian faith is true; otherwise our faith is in vain.

Question 2: This one is for Dr. Habermas. You were saying that Paul received the creed from an outside source. Is this one of the sources outside of the Bible that was possibly verified?

Habermas: Paul said, "I gave you what I was given," or "I delivered to you what I also received, how that Christ died for our sins according to the Scriptures, was buried, rose again on the third day, and appeared." Then he reproduced that list of appearances. This text is not Paul's—it's pre-Pauline. It's a piece of material that he took from somebody else and included in his book. By far, the most typical critical position is he received that material while he was in Jerusalem at about A.D. 35, or five years after the crucifixion. That's his testimony.

Questioner: Do we have any information about that source that he received the information from?

Habermas: Critical scholars take very seriously Paul's statement in Galatians 1:18-19 that he went up to Jerusalem just three years after his conversion, to meet with Peter and James the brother of Jesus. The immediate context concerns the gospel, which the New Testament defines repeatedly and clearly as including the resurrection. Just a few verses later, Paul tells us that he went back to Jerusalem fourteen years later, specifically to discuss the nature of the gospel [2:2]. The other apostles, Peter, James and John, agreed with his message and added nothing to it [2:6, 9]. As Paul said several years later, he and the other apostles were preaching the same message with regard to Jesus' resurrection [1 Cor 15:11]. So the consensus among scholars is that Paul probably received the creedal material when he visited Jerusalem the first time, which is the A.D. 35 date that I just mentioned. At the very least, from an exceptionally early date, these four major disciples discussed the nature of the gospel message and agreed on the details. This is rarely questioned by critical scholars. But note carefully, this is when Paul received and confirmed the message. The other apostles who passed it on to him had it before he did, and the events themselves are earlier still. So we are essentially back to the exact time when it all happened, as critical scholars have noted.

Question 3: [To Flew] I'm looking for a little clarification as far as evidence goes, for what constitutes evidence in ancient documents. It seems like Dr. Habermas has presented some sources to be considered from outside the text of the New Testament. And specifically speaking about the resurrection, I would think that an appearance would be made to somebody who was not a follower of Jesus at the time. And I would think that Saul of Tarsus would be considered one of those people to whom an appearance would be made. Such a radical change from his former lifestyle of persecution of the Jesus followers would be some form of evidence to me, but are there any outside sources from some other people to back up the claim that Saul was actually not a follower of Jesus?

Moderator: Is your question about the historical nature of Saul of Tarsus, or is your question to Flew about what sort of historical evidence he might count?

Questioner: Basically I guess the part about Paul. I'll go with him because that's what I'm having a problem with. It seems that Paul has presented his eyewitness account and then that's not good enough. Considering he wasn't a follower and then all of a sudden changed due to this appearance, I would think that that would hold some sway.

Flew: I'm not clear on what you're asking, but I think the worthwhile thing to say about this is that the evidence of Paul is certainly important and strong precisely because he was a convert. He was not a prior believer, and the evidence that he hadn't been previously a believer is about as clear as it could have been because he had been an active opponent. I think this has to be accepted as one of the most powerful bits of evidence that there is, precisely because he was converted by his vision, the nature of which I think is obscure. But still he was effectively converted by this from being an active opponent of the whole Christian movement.

Moderator: He concedes it as evidence, but it's just not convincing. It is striking, though, isn't it, that even someone like Saul, while not a prior believer, is someone who believes firmly in God, right?

Flew: I think that's very worthwhile to bring out. The evidence of Paul is the most powerful thing, apart from the fact that he was an outstanding philosophical mind, as the major Reformers were also.

Moderator: But an appearance to Pontius Pilate would have been cool. That would have been very nice.

Habermas: Yes, it would be, but I wonder: would that do it? I mean, I remember back in my days when I was searching, I told you I was arguing with Christians. I'd say, "If he appeared to Pilate, that would really be neat." Of course, he did appear to James, the brother of Jesus—you know, that's a family skeptic—versus an outsider. That's two skeptics who convert. But I remember having a skeptical episode where I looked out behind my house. There was this large tree, and I remember thinking to myself, "You know, if God really existed, he could knock that tree down." And I stood and I stared at it, and I said, "I thought so." Then I turned and walked away. Guess what? That night there was a storm and that tree was knocked down, and only that tree. For a few years I walked by that tree every day and it never, ever touched my skepticism. So I'm wondering, would that really have done it?

Moderator: Would it have convinced Antony Flew?

Habermas: I don't know.

Moderator: But you were convinced by the resurrection, by less than an appearance to Pontius Pilate. The evidence that you have is enough.

Habermas: You know what I'd like to see? I'd like for him [Flew] to see the resurrected Jesus.

Moderator: Well, I was going to ask that actually, about his own sense experience.

Habermas: By the way, folks, if you don't know this, Tony and I have been friends for almost twenty years. We've had a great few days here together, and everything I say teasingly I say respectfully. He is a good friend, and I really appreciate him.

Moderator: And they hardly ever come to blows. . . . The line for questioning is on—this one in the middle.

Question 4: This is to Dr. Habermas. You say that we have to pay attention to the evidence, and there's a lot of historical evidence that Jesus did rise. My question is also there's a lot of evidence this century that there was a boy found in Tibet who was the fourteenth reincarnation of Buddha. And there's a lot of evidence for that—that he passed a lot of tests that he couldn't have passed if he had not been the fourteenth reincarnation of Buddha. So how do we decide which factual *evidence* to believe?

Habermas: What would qualify as evidence for that claim?

Questioner: There's a story that he ran into a room and pointed at a chest of drawers and said, "My teeth are in there," and the teeth of the thirteenth Dalai Lama—his false teeth—were in there. They put him through a bunch of other rigorous tests.

Moderator: May I say that there are codified tests for proving that he is the fourteenth Dalai Lama?

Questioner: For proving that he is the fourteenth Dalai Lama . . . so my question is, if that's also factual evidence that would prove a different parallel religious universe, how do you know which historical evidence to take from?

Habermas: Good question. So you're talking about something like reincarnation, right? The leading reincarnation expert in the world is Ian Stevenson, a medical doctor and a professor at the University of Virginia. Your professor here, I think, used to know him, or at least studied there and knows of him. Stevenson has published several serious books on reincarnation, and he looks at all the data of cases like that: people who say, go to this town and make this right hand turn and make this one and you'll come to this little hut that looks like this. When he finished all his studies, Dr. Stevenson said that there are two theories that account for all the data: one is reincarnation, the other is a type of possession. He said they both account for all the data. So if we go back to the resurrection, it would seem to me you'd want to have an alternative that explains all the known data just as well.

Moderator: So your view is that the Dalai Lama is possessed?

Habermas: No, I've never met him. Thankfully, I can quote Ian Stevenson, and he says the data can be explained either way, and so I think that's not a close case if there are equal hypotheses.

Question 5: My question is for Dr. Flew. I haven't read any of your books, but I was wondering what made you argue against Jesus Christ or the God of Christianity instead of basing your philosophy against a Buddhist God or a Hindu God. What was your motivation for placing your argument against Christianity?

Moderator: Before he answers, I think he's an equal opportunity religious critic. [To Flew] The questioner was wondering why your focus is in her view anti-Christian, rather than anti-Hindu or Islam or something like that. I mean, part of the answer is, this is about the resurrection and so there's not much point in criticizing Buddhism for that, right?

Flew: Well, it's because this was the subject announced for the evening, but I will indulge myself a little. The much-respected supervisor of my graduate studies, Gilbert Ryle, whose work on the concept of mind some of you may have heard of, once said cheerfully, "Some of my colleagues think I'm prejudiced, but in my opinion there's nothing that rises in the east except the sun."

Question 6: My question is for Dr. Flew. As an atheist you believe that human beings have no soul; there's no afterlife. When we die, we simply cease to exist, right?

Flew: Yes, if I'm asked whether I believe in a future life. But whenever I think of the doctrine of hell and damnation, I'm a little uneasy. I don't accept the existence of a future life. I don't want a future life, thank you very much. And I don't even want a life of eternal bliss as it is described in most heavens, because it simply wouldn't appeal to me. You are asking what I believe, and I'm not being asked to give any reasons for my belief. Although my opinion about the ideas of the East is not necessarily the same as that of my supervisor's.

Questioner: So you'd rather take the chance that if you or anyone who dies is right, no matter what they believe, there are no consequences, no gain, versus the fact that, if Christians are right, when they die they gain eternal bliss with God in heaven and, when you die, there is eternal damnation waiting for you.

Moderator: I believe he wants to give Pascal's wager.

Flew: Oh yes, you want me to respond to Pascal's wager. I'm afraid at this time in the evening I don't feel fit to do so. I have recently written some second thoughts about this wager, but I don't recall them right now.

Habermas: At least he's honest.

Moderator: Is that your answer? He wants to know, all other things being equal, if there's a better payoff for having faith, then why not choose it?

Flew: Some people may be interested that this is actually an argument derived from Islam. It was something taken over by Pascal. Well, it's a powerful argument, I think, but for it to be effective, the idea of a future life has to be granted at the beginning, doesn't it? You are betting on the alternative possibilities of a future life in eternal torment, given to you by the predestinating God of traditional Christianity and Islam. This is not exactly what anyone would call a good God in any understanding, or any normal understanding of goodness, but still, yes, for the wager to be an effective challenge, the person who receives the wager has got to regard the hypothesis of a future life as a fairly live hypothesis, wouldn't they? Then they're challenged to take action to ensure that the future life is satisfactory, rather than the alternative.

And the idea of a future life is not one that should be taken as obviously a sound and coherent life, because human beings are creatures of flesh and blood. And what is supposed to survive? It is supposed to be an immaterial spirit that is in control of the human being. Well, this is not a basic, accepted fact; this is a notion held by some people and not by everyone, because they have been taught to believe it. It cannot be just taken as obviously being confronted with two equally reasonable betting options. You know Pascal offered the wager as a betting option; he was, in fact, a creator of some probability theories in his mathematician's life. Well, this isn't an option like making a bet on who's going to win a race when there's no doubt that there's going to be a race and there's no doubt as to who are the participants in the race. It is making a bet between two alternatives, both of which are based even for their intelligibility on a speculation. That's the best I can do for the moment.

Moderator: The issues involving pragmatic reasoning in Pascal's wager might be another topic for another panel perhaps. That's a good question, and that's probably not entirely satisfactory to you. You can talk to him later about it.

Question 7: My question is for Dr. Flew. If Jesus didn't rise from the dead, then what historically recorded evidence is there for the location of the body, or what happened to the body?

Flew: I don't know. I don't pretend to know. Because I don't think we can be in a position to know that the body was deposited in a tomb, though of course the opponents of Christianity wanted to find the body, didn't they? They wanted to find a body that hadn't risen.

Habermas: I thought you said earlier that we had enough basis, that those seven or eight reasons I gave were satisfactory for a burial?

Flew: Yes, I think they probably were satisfactory.

Habermas: So she wants to know, if we do have a burial, then what happened to the body? The tomb had to be open within days because it was right within the city, where people could just take a stroll and verify it or falsify it.

Flew: Well, I presume what happened to the body if it was buried—I don't know whether there's a different Christian view. Perhaps there is, and perhaps the view is that the body was resurrected.

Habermas: That's what Christians believe.

Moderator: She wants to know what you think.

Questioner: I mean, because you've been asking Dr. Habermas all night to show historical evidence and documented evidence that the body did resurrect, and he's quoted the Bible and he's quoted other texts. So is there any text or any person who has actually claimed that the body is or was still there afterward?

Moderator: May I say that I don't think that he disputed that historical evidence. I think his claim was that we agreed to this, but he didn't think it warranted the belief for him in the resurrection. He doesn't claim to have evidence that shows that the body was taken to Albuquerque or something. He's just saying, "I know what you're saying, and maybe it is rational for you to believe it, but it doesn't add up for me."

Question 8: My question is for Dr. Habermas. I am curious if Jesus claims to be the Son of God, and Christians accept that Jesus is the Son of God, in fact the second person of the Trinity. If I am correct, how miraculous is it really that he rose from the dead? I think what I'm asking is, as a Christian, should it be regarded as a miracle that the Son of God, or the second person of the Godhead, rose from the dead to begin with?

Moderator: So it's not a miracle, because it is what you expect?

Habermas: This is the Christian naturalistic theory for the resurrection. Seriously, suppose you were in the countryside leaving your first-century shop and going to hear Jesus speak on a sunny afternoon. You hear him preach, and he makes some extraordinary claims, and these claims don't seem to be computing. I mean, it's not every day that you bump into the Son of God, right? So this fellow claims to be the Son of God, and that is rather extraordinary. When you hear his claims, you're not a Christian. I mean, for the most part, these folks are listening, and they're probably going back to their shops, scratching their heads and thinking this fellow is really something.

As Dr. Flew said today, Jesus was an incredibly charismatic figure, and people thought he was fantastic. Over and over again, the Gospels say he spoke as somebody who had wisdom, not as one of the religious leaders they'd heard. So they were impressed with him, but nonetheless I think they're going back to their shops, scratching their heads, saying, "I don't know what to make of this fellow."

Then somebody comes to your shop a few months later and says, "Hey, did you hear that the Galilean is dead? Yeah, the Romans killed him." Oh man, what do I think now? You go back to work in your shop.

But two weeks later, someone says, "Hey, did you hear? The Galilean that you went to hear speak was raised from the dead! That big fisherman, Peter, is coming to town today. I think we should go hear him speak."

I think many of these folks were very skeptical when they first heard Jesus' message, but what closed the argument for those who believed? What closed the argument for them was the resurrection. I don't think it made sense to many of them until they got all the puzzle pieces put together. And the resurrection is what put all the puzzle pieces together. I don't know if that answers your question or not.

Question 9: Okay, my question is directed to Gary Habermas. And my question is, you guys talked a little bit about the idea of having tangible evidence of the resurrection like the video camera, but if God does exist, wouldn't he provide some kind of tangible evidence so we would not have to have this argument in the first place? And then also in addition to that, if I believe correctly, a major idea of Christianity is this idea of faith, and doesn't the idea of having the resurrection occur sort of contradict that idea of having faith in God at the same time?

Habermas: I understand the faith part, but what was the first part of your question?

Questioner: The first part of my question was, if God exists, wouldn't he provide some kind of tangible evidence?

Habermas: Sure, I mean he doesn't have to, but if God exists I would think that providing tangible evidence is one very important way he could act, so when we see that in history we think, "Wow, he's acted." I mean, that's precisely what they think. Now, as far as your question about faith, that's a great question. Perhaps I'm not taking you correctly, but I'm hearing something like this: Isn't Christianity about faith, and you're sitting here talking about evidence all night. How do you relate faith to evidence?

Questioner: Well, talking specifically about the resurrection, you mentioned several times in your argument that a purpose of the resurrection was to show that Jesus was the Son of God. You mentioned it just now in your story of the Jewish shopkeeper. It was used as evidence that he existed, but doesn't that contradict the idea of having faith in God?

Habermas: Okay, let me give you another example. You date somebody and, after a while, you think you know this person better than anyone else on the face of the Earth. But you're still not married unless you say, "I do." Perhaps you do know them better than anyone else, but you still must say, "I do."

I think that's an analogy to Christianity. When people come to Christ, they're saying "I do" to Jesus. I don't think there's any conflict between my knowing somebody real well and then thinking, "You know what, you're the kind of person with whom I would like to spend the rest of my life." But now it takes a commitment. Don't I realize that half the marriages in this country break up? Don't I know that this person might not be what they seem? You know, there are all kinds of objections. But I may still say, "Let's do it. Would you marry me?"

I think it's very similar with faith. Just because you have all your ducks in a row doesn't mean there's nothing that can disturb this. You can still have doubts or other issues, and obviously this happens to marriages too. So I think you try to be really careful, you try to line your data up, and you can decide if you want to say "I do" to Jesus Christ. That "I do" step, that faith, that commitment, is not contradicted by the fact that you thought through everything first. In fact, we say the opposite—we say that the person who was careful on the front end and who then takes a step is smarter than the person who makes a fast decision, whether it is faith or marriage. So I don't think there needs to be any conflict whatsoever between evidence and faith. We still have to invoke the commitment portion.

Question 10: Okay, the disciples were all Jews with Jewish teaching, and isn't Jewish belief that the Messiah would have been an earthly Messiah, someone to set up some kind of worldly kingdom?

And to my knowledge, the idea of a resurrection was never taught in
the Old Testament. So what sort of a resurrection would give the
disciples the idea?

Habermas: I think you're largely correct. Probably the most common Jewish view was that a king would come and set up God's kingdom, which he'd set up on behalf of the God of the universe. Interestingly enough, in Daniel 7:13-14, this person is one like a Son of Man,
and he is separate from the person Christians call God the Father
because, in the same context, the latter is called the Ancient of Days.[19]
But the Son of Man goes to Earth to set up the kingdom. Very interestingly, this was Jesus' favorite self-designation. He called himself
the Son of Man more than any other title.

There's a lot of content here that I'm not going to be able to mention, but personally I think that Jesus' use of the Son of Man title
comes very close to who the Son of God is: I think they are two angles on the same person, and both are indications of a claim to deity.
Maybe that doesn't help you, but I'm saying, yes, the disciples apparently held your view and they thought Jesus was fulfilling it. But
Jesus took the kingdom teaching in a different direction. As Jesus
said, it was not just an earthly kingdom, but God's rule both on
earth as well as in heaven. You might say that the resurrection initi-
ated both stages.

Question 11: Sort of going in the same vein of video evidence,
video is pretty good evidence versus written evidence. It seems like
our ability to provide more authentic proofs, such as video proof,
might be better than a person saying I saw somebody throw a foot-
ball and score a touchdown. Recent audio or video records are hard
to refute, but it seems, when it comes to something like the Bible,
there's less and less evidence as time advances.

---

[19]Daniel 7:13-14 (NASB): "I kept looking . . . and behold, with the clouds of heaven one like
a Son of Man was coming, and he came up to the Ancient of Days and was presented
before him. And to him was given dominion, glory, and a kingdom . . . his dominion is
an everlasting dominion which will not pass away."

Moderator: Or perhaps as an alternative, if the resurrection happened now and we caught it on MTV . . .

Habermas: That would be pretty neat, and again I have those in the back—photographs of the Shroud of Turin, the most investigated archaeological artifact in history. Some think it is a sort of photo of Jesus' resurrection. Seriously, I didn't bring those here. But for good or for ill, we're dealing with an ancient historical event. And in ancient history, we can only deal with the tools we have. Let me give you an example. We use the phrase "Julius Caesar crossing the Rubicon," and we often say that to indicate a really sure event. But there are very few firsthand reports in the ancient world for Julius Caesar crossing the Rubicon River. Multiple sources increase the likelihood of reliability. Obviously, we didn't have a video camera there, but the data you do have, you have to deal with it, and that's how ancient history is done. No one's going to throw ancient history out the window, so you must deal with what you have.

PART II

Antony Flew's Journey to Theism

My Pilgrimage from Atheism to Theism

A Discussion Between Antony Flew and Gary Habermas

ANTONY FLEW AND GARY HABERMAS MET in February 1985 in Dallas.[1] The occasion was a series of debates between atheists and theists, featuring many influential philosophers, scientists and other scholars.[2]

In May of that year, Flew and Habermas debated at Liberty University before a large audience. The topic that night was the resurrection of Jesus.[3] Although Flew was arguably the world's foremost philosophical atheist, he had intriguingly also earned the distinction of being one of the chief philosophical commentators on the topic of miracles.[4] Habermas specialized in the subject of Jesus' resurrec-

---

[1]Material in this section originally appeared as Antony Flew and Gary Habermas, "My Pilgrimage from Atheism to Theism: A Discussion Between Antony Flew and Gary Habermas," *Philosophia Christi* 6 (2004): 197-211; Gary R. Habermas, "Antony Flew's Deism Revisited: A Review Essay on *There Is a God*," *Philosophia Christi* 9, no.2 (Winter 2007): 431-41. Used by permission of *Philosophia Christi* and the Evangelical Philosophical Society <www.epsociety.org>.

[2]"Christianity Challenges the University: An International Conference of Theists and Atheists," Dallas, February 7-10, 1985, organized by Roy Abraham Varghese.

[3]See Gary R. Habermas and Antony G. N. Flew, *Did Jesus Rise from the Dead? The Resurrection Debate*, ed. Terry L. Miethe (San Francisco: Harper & Row, 1987).

[4]Some examples by Antony Flew include "Miracles and Methodology," in his *Hume's Philosophy of Belief: A Study of His First Inquiry* (London: Routledge and Kegan Paul, 1961); "The Credentials of Revelation: Miracle and History," in his *God and Philosophy* (New York: Dell, 1966); "Miracles," in *Encyclopedia of Philosophy,* ed. Paul Edwards (New

tion.[5] Thus, the ensuing dialogue on the historical evidence for the central Christian claim was a natural outgrowth of their research.

Over the next twenty years, Flew and Habermas developed a friendship, writing dozens of letters, talking often, and dialoguing twice more on the resurrection. In April 2000 they participated in a live debate on the Inspiration Television Network, moderated by John Ankerberg.[6] In January 2003 they again dialogued on the resurrection at California Polytechnic State University, San Luis Obispo.[7]

During a couple of telephone discussions shortly after their last dialogue, Flew explained to Habermas that he was considering becoming a theist. While Flew did not change his position at that time, he concluded that certain philosophical and scientific considerations were causing him to do some serious rethinking. He characterized his position as that of atheism standing in tension with several huge question marks.

Then, a year later, in January 2004, Flew informed Habermas that he had indeed become a theist. While still rejecting the concept of special revelation, whether Christian, Jewish or Islamic, nonetheless he had concluded that theism was true. In Flew's words, he simply

---

York: Macmillan, 1967); "The Impossibility of the Miraculous," in David Hume, *Philosophy of Religion* (Winston-Salem, N.C.: Wake Forest University Press, 1985); "Introduction," in David Hume, *Of Miracles,* (LaSalle, Ill.: Open Court, 1985); "Neo-Humean Arguments about the Miraculous," in *In Defense of Miracles: A Comprehensive Case for God's Action in History*, ed., R. Douglas Geivett and Gary R. Habermas (Downers Grove, Ill.: InterVarsity Press, 1997).

[5]Some examples by Gary Habermas include *The Risen Jesus and Future Hope* (Lanham, Md.: Rowman and Littlefield, 2003); *The Historical Jesus: Ancient Evidence for the Life of Christ* (Joplin, Mo.: College Press, 1996); *The Resurrection of Jesus: An Apologetic* (Lanham, Md.: University Press of America, 1984); "Knowing that Jesus' Resurrection Occurred: A Response to Stephen Davis," *Faith and Philosophy* 2 (1985): 295-302; "Resurrection Claims in Non-Christian Religions," *Religious Studies* 25 (1989): 167-77; "The Late Twentieth-Century Resurgence of Naturalistic Responses to Jesus' Resurrection," *Trinity Journal* 22 (2001): 179-96. For a more popular treatment, see Habermas and Michael R. Licona, *The Case for the Resurrection of Jesus* (Grand Rapids: Kregel, 2004).

[6]Gary R. Habermas and Antony G. N. Flew, *Resurrected? An Atheist and Theist Debate*, ed. John Ankerberg (Lanham, Md.: Rowman and Littlefield, 2005).

[7]Reprinted here with permission of The Veritas Forum.

"had to go where the evidence leads."[8]

The following interview took place in early 2004 and was subsequently modified by both participants throughout the year. This nontechnical discussion sought to engage Flew over the course of several topics that reflect his move from atheism to theism. The chief purpose was not to pursue the details of any particular issue, so we bypassed many avenues that would have presented a plethora of other intriguing questions and responses. These were often tantalizingly ignored, left to ripen for another discussion. Neither did we try to persuade each other of alternate positions.

Our singular purpose was simply to explore and report Flew's new position, allowing him to explain various aspects of his pilgrimage. We thought that this in itself was a worthy goal. Along the way, an additional benefit emerged, as Flew reminisced about various moments from his childhood, graduate studies and career.

Habermas: Tony, you recently told me that you have come to believe in the existence of God. Would you comment on that?

Flew: Well, I don't believe in the God of any revelatory system, although I am open to that. But it seems to me that the case for an Aristotelian God, who has the characteristics of power and also intelligence, is now much stronger than it ever was before. And it was from Aristotle that Aquinas drew the materials for producing his five ways of, hopefully, proving the existence of God. Aquinas took them, reasonably enough, to prove, if they proved anything, the existence of the God of the Christian revelation. But Aristotle himself never produced a definition of the word *god*, which is a curious fact. But this concept still led to the basic outline of the five ways. It seems to me that, from the existence of Aristotle's God, you can't infer anything about human behavior. So what Aristotle had to say about justice (justice, of course, as conceived by the founding fathers of the American Republic as opposed to the "social" justice of John Rawls[9])

---

[8]Telephone conversation with Gary Habermas, September 9, 2004.
[9]John Rawls, *A Theory of Justice* (Cambridge, Mass.: Harvard University Press, 1971).

was very much a human idea, and he thought that this idea of justice was what ought to govern the behavior of individual human beings in their relations with others.

Habermas: Once you mentioned to me that your view might be called Deism. Do you think that would be a fair designation?

Flew: Yes, absolutely right. What Deists, such as Mr. Jefferson, who drafted the American Declaration of Independence, believed was that, while reason, mainly in the form of arguments to design, assures us that there is a God, there is no room either for any supernatural revelation of that God or for any transactions between that God and individual human beings.

Habermas: Then would you comment on your "openness" to the notion of theistic revelation?

Flew: Yes. I am open to it, but not enthusiastic about potential revelation from God. On the positive side, for example, I am very much impressed with physicist Gerald Schroeder's comments on Genesis 1.[10] That this biblical account might be scientifically accurate raises the possibility that it is revelation.

Habermas: You very kindly noted that our debates and discussions had influenced your move in the direction of theism.[11] You mentioned that this initial influence contributed in part to your comment that naturalistic efforts have never succeeded in producing "a plausible conjecture as to how any of these complex molecules might have evolved from simple entities."[12] Then in your recently rewritten introduction to the forthcoming edition of your classic volume *God and Philosophy*, you say that the original version of that book is now obsolete. You mention a number of trends in theistic argumentation that you find convincing, like big bang cosmology,

---

[10]Gerald L. Schroeder, *The Science of God: The Convergence of Scientific and Biblical Wisdom* (New York: Broadway Books, 1998).

[11]Letter from Antony Flew, November 9, 2000.

[12]Antony Flew, "God and the Big Bang" (lecture, 2000), pp. 5-6; this is a lecture commemorating the 140th anniversary of the British Association meeting regarding Charles Darwin's *The Origin of the Species*.

fine-tuning and Intelligent Design arguments. Which arguments for God's existence did you find most persuasive?

Flew: I think that the most impressive arguments for God's existence are those that are supported by recent scientific discoveries. I've never been much impressed by the Kalam cosmological argument, and I don't think it has gotten any stronger recently. However, I think the argument to Intelligent Design is enormously stronger than it was when I first met it.

Habermas: So you like arguments such as those that proceed from big bang cosmology and fine-tuning arguments?

Flew: Yes.

Habermas: You also recently told me that you do not find the moral argument to be very persuasive. Is that right?

Flew: That's correct. It seems to me that for a strong moral argument, you've got to have God as the justification of morality. To do this makes doing the morally good a purely prudential matter rather than, as the moral philosophers of my youth used to call it, a good in itself. (Compare the classic discussion of Plato's Euthyphro.)

Habermas: So take C. S. Lewis's argument for morality as presented in *Mere Christianity*.[13] You didn't find that to be very impressive?

Flew: No, I didn't. Perhaps I should mention that, when I was in college, I attended fairly regularly the weekly meetings of C. S. Lewis's Socratic Club. In all my time at Oxford, these meetings were chaired by Lewis. I think he was by far the most powerful of Christian apologists for the sixty or more years following his founding of that club. As late as the 1970s, I used to find that, in the U.S.A., in at least half of the campus bookstores of the universities and liberal arts colleges which I visited, there was at least one long shelf devoted to his very various published works.

Habermas: Although you disagreed with him, did you find him to

---

[13]C. S. Lewis, *Mere Christianity* (New York: Macmillan, 1980), esp. bk. 1.

be a very reasonable sort of fellow?

Flew: Oh yes, very much so, an eminently reasonable man.

Habermas: And what do you think about the ontological argument for the existence of God?

Flew: All my later thinking and writing about philosophy was greatly influenced by my year of postgraduate study under the supervision of Gilbert Ryle, the then professor of metaphysical philosophy in the University of Oxford, as well as the editor of *Mind*. It was the very year in which his enormously influential work *The Concept of Mind* was first published.[14] I was told that in the years between the wars whenever another version of the ontological argument was raised, Gilbert forthwith set himself to refute it.

My own initial lack of enthusiasm for the ontological argument developed into strong repulsion when I realized from reading the *Theodicy* of Leibniz[15] that it was the identification of the concept of Being with the concept of Goodness (which ultimately derives from Plato's identification in *The Republic* of the Form or Idea of the Good with the Form or the Idea of the Real), which enabled Leibniz in his *Theodicy* validity to conclude that a universe in which most human beings are predestined to an eternity of torture is the "best of all possible worlds."

Habermas: So of the major theistic arguments, such as the cosmological, teleological, moral and ontological, the only really impressive ones that you take to be decisive are the scientific forms of teleology?

Flew: Absolutely. It seems to me that Richard Dawkins constantly overlooks the fact that Darwin himself, in the fourteenth chapter of *The Origin of Species*, pointed out that his whole argument began with a being that already possessed reproductive powers. This is the creature the evolution of which a truly comprehensive theory of evolution must give some account. Darwin himself was well aware that

---

[14]Gilbert Ryle, *The Concept of Mind* (London: Hutchinson, 1948).

[15]Gottfried W. Leibniz, *Theodicy*, ed. A. Farrer, trans. E. M. Huggard (1710; reprint, London: Routledge, 1965).

he had not produced such an account. It now seems to me that the findings of more than fifty years of DNA research have provided materials for a new and enormously powerful argument to design.

Habermas: As I recall, you also refer to this in the new introduction to your *God and Philosophy*.

Flew: Yes, I do; or, since the book has not yet been published, I will!

Habermas: Since you affirm Aristotle's concept of God, do you think we can also affirm Aristotle's implications that the First Cause hence knows all things?

Flew: I suppose we should say this: I'm not at all sure what one should think concerning some of these very fundamental issues. There does seem to be a reason for a First Cause, but I'm not at all sure how much we have to explain here. What idea of God is necessary to provide an explanation of the existence of the universe and all which is in it?

Habermas: If God is the First Cause, what about omniscience, or omnipotence?

Flew: Well, the First Cause, if there was a First Cause, has very clearly produced everything that is going on. I suppose that does imply creation "in the beginning."

Habermas: In the same introduction, you also make a comparison between Aristotle's God and Spinoza's God. Are you implying, with some interpreters of Spinoza, that God is pantheistic?

Flew: I'm noting there that *God and Philosophy* has become out of date and should now be seen as an historical document rather than as a direct contribution to current discussion. I'm sympathetic to Spinoza because he makes some statements which seem to me correctly to describe the human situation. But for me the most important thing about Spinoza is not what he says, but what he does not say. He does not say that God has any preferences either about or any intentions concerning human behavior or about the eternal destinies of human beings.

Habermas: What role might your love for the writings of David

Hume play in a discussion about the existence of God? Do you have any new insights on Hume, given your new belief in God?

Flew: No, not really.

Habermas: Do you think Hume ever answers the questions of God?

Flew: I think of him as, shall we say, an unbeliever. But it's interesting to note that he himself was perfectly willing to accept one of the conditions of his appointment, if he had been appointed to a chair of philosophy at the University of Edinburgh. That condition was, roughly speaking, to provide some sort of support and encouragement for people performing prayers and executing other acts of worship. I believe that Hume thought that the institution of religious belief could be, and in his day and place was, socially beneficial.[16]

I too, having been brought up as a Methodist, have always been aware of the possible and in many times and places actual benefit of objective religious instruction. It is now several decades since I first tried to draw attention to the danger of relying on a modest amount of compulsory religious instruction in schools to meet the need for moral education, especially in a period of relentlessly declining religious belief. But all such warnings by individuals were, of course, ignored. So we now have in the United Kingdom a situation in which any mandatory requirements to instruct pupils in state-funded schools in the teachings of the established or any other religion are widely ignored. The only official attempt to construct a secular substitute was vitiated by the inability of the moral philosopher on the relevant government committee to recognize the fundamental difference between justice without prefix or suffix and the "social" justice of John Rawls's *A Theory of Justice.*

I must sometime send you a copy of the final chapter of my latest and presumably last book, in which I offer a syllabus and a program

---

[16]See Donald W. Livingston, *Philosophical Melancholy and Delirium: Hume's Pathology of Philosophy* (Chicago: University of Chicago Press, 1998), p. 150.

for moral education in secular schools.[17] This is relevant and important for both the United States and the United Kingdom. To the United States because the Supreme Court has utterly misinterpreted the clause in the Constitution about not establishing a religion: misunderstanding it as imposing a ban on all official reference to religion. In the United Kingdom any effective program or moral education has to be secular because unbelief is now very widespread.

Habermas: In *God and Philosophy* and in many other places in our discussions too, it seems that your primary motivation for rejecting theistic arguments used to be the problem of evil. In terms of your new belief in God, how do you now conceptualize God's relationship to the reality of evil in the world?

Flew: Well, absent revelation, why should we perceive anything as objectively evil? The problem of evil is a problem only for Christians. For Muslims everything which human beings perceive as evil, just as much as everything we perceive as good, has to be obediently accepted as produced by the will of Allah. I supposed that the moment when, as a schoolboy of fifteen years, it first appeared to me that the thesis that the universe was created and is sustained by a Being of infinite power and goodness is flatly incompatible with the occurrence of massive undeniable and undenied evils in that universe was the first step toward my future career as a philosopher. It was, of course, very much later that I learned of the philosophical identification of goodness with existence.

Habermas: In your view, then, God hasn't done anything about evil.

Flew: No, not at all, other than producing a lot of it.

Habermas: Given your theism, what about mind-body issues?

Flew: I think those who want to speak about an afterlife have got to meet the difficulty of formulating a concept of an incorporeal person. Here I have again to refer back to my year as a graduate student

---

[17]Antony Flew, *Social Life and Moral Judgment* (New Brunswick, N.H.: Transaction, 2003).

supervised by Gilbert Ryle, in the year in which he published *The Concept of Mind*.

At that time there was considerable comment, usually hostile, in the serious British press, on what was called Oxford Linguistic Philosophy. The objection was usually that this involved a trivialization of a very profound and important discipline.

I was by this moved to give a talk to the Philosophy Postgraduates Club under the title "Matter Which Matters." In it I argued that, so far from ignoring what Immanuel Kant described as the three great problems of philosophers—God, Freedom and Immortality—the linguistic approach promised substantial progress toward their solution.

I myself always intended to make contributions in all those three areas. Indeed my first philosophical publication was relevant to the third.[18] Indeed it was not very long after I got my first job as a professional philosopher that I confessed to Ryle that if ever I was asked to deliver the Gifford Lectures I would give them under the title "The Logic of Mortality."[19] They were an extensive argument to the conclusion that it is simply impossible to create a concept of an incorporeal spirit.

Habermas: Is such a concept necessarily required for the notion of an afterlife?

Flew: Dr. Johnson's dictionary defines death as the soul leaving the body. If the soul is to be, as Dr. Johnson and almost—if perhaps not quite—everyone else in his day believed it to be, something which can sensibly be said to leave its present residence and to take up or be forced to take up residence elsewhere, then a soul must be, in the philosophical sense, a substance rather than merely a characteristic of something else.

My Gifford Lectures were published after Richard Swinburne published his, *The Evolution of the Soul*.[20] So when mine were reprinted

---

[18]Antony Flew, "Selves," *Mind* (1949): 355-58.
[19]Antony Flew, *The Logic of Mortality* (Oxford: Blackwell, 1987).
[20]Richard Swinburne, *The Evolution of the Soul* (Oxford: Clarendon, 1986).

under the title *Merely Mortal? Can You Survive Your Own Death?*[21] I might have been expected to respond to any criticisms which Swinburne had made of my earlier publications in the same area. But the embarrassing truth is that he had taken no notice of any previous relevant writings either by me or by anyone published since World War II. There would not have been much point in searching for books or articles before that date since Swinburne and I had been the only Gifford lecturers to treat the question of a future life for the sixty years past. Even more remarkably, Swinburne in his Gifford Lectures ignored Bishop Butler's decisive observation: "Memory may reveal but cannot constitute personal identity."[22]

Habermas: On several occasions, you and I have dialogued regarding the subject of near-death experiences, especially the specific sort where people have reported verifiable data from a distance away from themselves. Sometimes these reports even occur during the absence of heartbeat or brain waves.[23] After our second dialogue you wrote me a letter and said, "I find the materials about near death experiences so challenging. . . . This evidence equally certainly weakens if it does not completely refute my argument against doctrines of a future life."[24] In light of these evidential near-death cases, what do you think about the possibility of an afterlife, especially given your theism?

Flew: An incorporeal being may be hypothesized, and hypothesized to possess a memory. But before we could rely on its memory even of its own experiences, we should need to be able to provide an account of how this hypothesized incorporeal being could be identified in the first place and then—after what lawyers call an affluxion of time—reidentified even by himself or herself as one and the same individual

---

[21]Antony Flew, *Merely Mortal? Can You Survive Your Own Death?* (Amherst, N.Y.: Prometheus, 2000).

[22]Joseph Butler, *Works*, ed. W. E. Gladstone (Oxford: Clarendon, 1896), 1:387.

[23]For many cases, see Gary R. Habermas and J. P. Moreland, *Beyond Death: Exploring the Evidence for Immortality* (Wheaton, Ill.: Crossway, 1998), chaps. 7-9.

[24]Letter from Antony Flew, September 6, 2000.

spiritual being. Until we have evidence that we have been and presumably—as Dr. Johnson and so many lesser men have believed—are to be identified with such incorporeal spirits, I do not see why near-death experiences should be taken as evidence for the conclusion that human beings will enjoy a future life or—more likely, if either of the two great revealed religions is true—suffer eternal torment.

Habermas: I agree that near-death experiences do not evidence the doctrines of either heaven or hell. But do you think these evidential cases increase the possibility of some sort of an afterlife, again, given your theism?

Flew: I still hope and believe there's no possibility of an afterlife.

Habermas: Even though you hope there's no afterlife, what do you think of the evidence that there might be such, as perhaps indicated by these evidential near-death cases? And even if there is no clear notion of what sort of body might be implied here, do you find this evidence helpful in any way? In other words, apart from the form in which a potential afterlife might take, do you still find these to be evidence for something?

Flew: It's puzzling to offer an interpretation of these experiences. But I presume it has got to be taken as extrasensory perceiving by the flesh-and-blood person who is the subject of the experiences in question. What it cannot be is the hypothesized incorporeal spirit which you would wish to identify with the person who nearly died, but actually did not. For this concept of an incorporeal spirit cannot properly be assumed to have been given sense until and unless some means has been provided for identifying such spirits in the first place and reidentifying them as one and the same individual incorporeal spirits after the affluxion of time. Until and unless this has been done, we have always to remember Bishop Butler's objection: "Memory may reveal but cannot constitute personal identity."

Perhaps I should here point out that, long before I took my first university course in philosophy, I was much interested in what in the United Kingdom, where it began, is still called psychical research, although the term *parapsychology* is now used almost everywhere else. Perhaps I ought here to confess that my first book was brashly entitled *A New Approach to Psychical Research*,[25] and my interest in this subject continued for many years thereafter.

Habermas: Actually you have also written to me that these near-death experiences "certainly constitute impressive evidence for the possibility of the occurrence of human consciousness independent of any occurrences in the human brain."[26]

Flew: When I came to consider what seemed to me the most impressive of these near-death cases, I asked myself, what is the traditional first question to ask about "psychic" phenomena? It is, "When, where and by whom were the phenomena first reported?" Some people seem to confuse near-death experiences with after-death experiences. Where any such near-death experiences become relevant to the question of a future life is when and only when they appear to show "the occurrence of human consciousness independent of any occurrences in the human brain."

Habermas: Elsewhere you again very kindly noted my influence on your thinking here regarding these data being decent evidence for human consciousness independent of "electrical activity in the brain."[27] If some near-death experiences are evidenced, independently confirmed experiences during a near-death state, even in persons whose heart or brain may not be functioning, isn't that quite impressive evidence? Are near-death experiences, then, the best evidence for an afterlife?

Flew: Oh, yes, certainly. They are basically the only evidence.

Habermas: What critical evaluation would you make of the three major monotheisms? Are there any particular philosophical strengths or weaknesses in Christianity, Judaism or Islam?

---

[25]Antony Flew, *A New Approach to Psychical Research* (London: C. A. Watts, 1953).

[26]Letter from Antony Flew, September 6, 2000.

[27]Antony Flew, "God and the Big Bang," p. 2. Habermas's influence on Flew's statement here is noted in Flew's letter of November 9, 2000 (also note 11 above).

Flew: If all I knew or believed about God was what I might have learned from Aristotle, then I should have assumed that everything in the universe, including human conduct, was exactly as God wanted it to be. And this is indeed the case, in so far as both Christianity and Islam are predestinarian, a fundamental teaching of both religious systems. What was true of Christianity in the Middle Ages is certainly no longer equally true after the Reformation. But Islam has neither suffered nor enjoyed either a Reformation or an Enlightenment. In the *Summa Theologiae* we may read:

> As men are ordained to eternal life throughout the providence of God, it likewise is part of that providence to permit some to fall away from that end; this is called reprobation. . . . Reprobation implies not only foreknowledge but also is something more.[28]

What and how much that something more is, the *Summa Contra Gentiles* makes clear:

> Just as God not only gave being to things when they first began, but is also—as the conserving cause of being—the cause of their being as long as they last. . . . Every operation, therefore, of anything is traced back to Him as its cause.[29]

The Angelic Doctor, however, is always the devotedly complacent apparatchik. He sees no problem about the justice of either the inflicting of infinite and everlasting penalties for finite and temporal offences, or of their affliction upon creatures for offences which their Creator makes them freely choose to commit. Thus, the Angelic Doctor assures us:

> In order that the happiness of the saints may be more delightful to them and that they may render more copious thanks to God . . . they are allowed to see perfectly the sufferings of the

---

[28]Thomas Aquinas *Summa Theologiae* 1, q. 23, a. 3.
[29]Thomas Aquinas *Summa Contra Gentiles* 3.67.

damned. . . . Divine justice and their own deliverance will be
the direct cause of the joy of the blessed, while the pains of the
damned will cause it indirectly . . . the blessed in glory will
have no pity for the damned.[30]

The statements of predestinarianism in the Qur'an are much more
aggressive and unequivocal than even the strongest in the Bible.
Compare the following from the Qur'an with that from Romans 9.

As for the unbelievers, alike it is to them
Whether thou hast warned them or hast not warned them
They do not believe.[31]

God has set a seal on their hearts and on the hearing
And on the eyes is a covering
And there awaits them a mighty chastisement.[32]

In the United Kingdom the doctrine of hell has for the last century
or more been progressively deemphasized, until in 1995 it was explicitly and categorically abandoned by the Church of England. It
would appear that the Roman Catholic Church has not abandoned
either the doctrine of hell nor predestination.

Thomas Hobbes spent a very large part of the forty years between
the first publication of the King James Bible and the first publication
of his own *Leviathan* engaged in biblical criticism, one very relevant
finding of which I now quote:

And it is said besides in many places [that the wicked] shall go
into everlasting fire; and that the worm of conscience never
dieth; and all this is comprehended in the word everlasting
death, which is ordinarily interpreted everlasting life in torments. And yet I can find nowhere that any man shall live in
torments everlastingly. Also, it seemeth hard to say that God

---

[30]Thomas Aquinas *Summa Theologiae* 3, supp. 94, a. 1-3.
[31]Arthur J. Arberry, trans., Qur'an 2 (Oxford: Oxford University Press, 1998).
[32]Qur'an 5.

who is the father of mercies; that doth in heaven and earth all
that he will, that hath the hearts of all men in his disposing;
that worketh in men both to do, and to will; and without whose
free gift a man hath neither inclination to good, nor repentance
of evil, should punish men's transgressions without any end of
time, and with all the extremity of torture, that men can imagine and more.[33]

As for Islam, it is, I think, best described in a Marxian way as the
uniting and justifying ideology of Arab imperialism. Between the
New Testament and the Qur'an there is (as it is customary to say
when making such comparisons) no comparison. Whereas markets
can be found for books on reading the Bible as literature, to read the
Qur'an is a penance rather than a pleasure. There is no order or development in its subject matter. All the chapters (*suras*) are arranged
in order of their length, with the longest at the beginning. However,
since the Qur'an consists in a collection of bits and pieces of putative
revelation delivered to the prophet Muhammad by the archangel Ga-
briel in classical Arabic on many separate but unknown occasions, it
is difficult to suggest any superior principle of organization.

One point about the editing of the Qur'an is rarely made, although
it would appear to be of very substantial theological significance.
Every sura is prefaced by the words "In the Name of God, the Merci-
ful, the Compassionate." Yet there are references to hell on at least
255 of the 669 pages of Arberry's rendering of the Qur'an,[34] and quite
often pages have two such references.

Whereas the apostle Paul, who was the chief contributor to the
New Testament, knew all the three relevant languages and obviously
possessed a first-class philosophical mind, the Prophet, though
gifted in the arts of persuasion and clearly a considerable military

---

[33]Thomas Hobbes, *Leviathan*, ed. J. C. A. Gaskin (Oxford: Oxford University Press, 1998),
   p. 416.
[34]This is the interpretive version by Arthur Arberry, in the Oxford University Press
   edition.

leader, was both doubtfully literate and certainly ill informed about the contents of the Old Testament and about several matters of which God, if not even the least informed of the Prophet's contemporaries, must have been cognizant.

This raises the possibility of what my philosophical contemporaries in the heyday of Gilbert Ryle would have described as a knockdown falsification of Islam: something which is most certainly not possible in the case of Christianity. If I do eventually produce such a paper, it will obviously have to be published anonymously.

Habermas: What do you think about the Bible?

Flew: The Bible is a work which someone who had not the slightest concern about the question of the truth or falsity of the Christian religion could read as people read the novels of the best novelists. It is an eminently readable book.

Habermas: You and I have had three dialogues on the resurrection of Jesus. Are you any closer to thinking that the resurrection could have been a historical fact?

Flew: No, I don't think so. The evidence for the resurrection is better than for claimed miracles in any other religion. It's outstandingly different in quality and quantity, I think, from the evidence offered for the occurrence of most other supposedly miraculous events. But you must remember that I approached it after considerable reading of reports of psychical research and its criticisms. This showed me how quickly evidence of remarkable and supposedly miraculous events can be discredited.

What the psychical researcher looks for is evidence from witnesses of the supposedly paranormal events recorded as soon as possible after their occurrence. What we do not have is evidence from anyone who was in Jerusalem at the time, who witnessed one of the allegedly miraculous events and recorded his or her testimony immediately after the occurrence of that allegedly miraculous event. In the 1950s and 1960s I heard several suggestions from hard-bitten young Australian and American philosophers of conceivable miracles the actual occurrence of which, it was contended, no one could have overlooked or denied. Why, they asked, if God wanted to be recognized and worshiped, did God not produce a miracle of this unignorable and undeniable kind?

Habermas: So you think that, for a miracle, the evidence for Jesus' resurrection is better than other miracle claims?

Flew: Oh yes, I think so. It's much better, for example, than that for most—if not all—of the, so to speak, run-of-the-mill Roman Catholic miracles. On this see, for instance, D. J. West's *Eleven Lourdes Miracles.*

Habermas: You have made numerous comments over the years that Christians are justified in their beliefs such as Jesus' resurrection or other major tenets of their faith. In our last two dialogues I think you even remarked that for someone who is already a Christian there are many good reasons to believe Jesus' resurrection. Would you comment on that?

Flew: Yes, certainly. This is an important matter about rationality which I have fairly recently come to appreciate. What it is rational for any individual to believe about some matter which is fresh to that individual's consideration depends on what he or she rationally believed before being confronted with this fresh situation. For suppose they rationally believed in the existence of a God of any revelation, then it would be entirely reasonable for them to see the fine-tuning argument as providing substantial confirmation of their belief in the existence of that God.

Habermas: You've told me that you have a very high regard for John and Charles Wesley and their traditions. What accounts for your appreciation?

Flew: The greatest thing is their tremendous achievement of creating the Methodist movement mainly among the working class. Methodism made it impossible to build a really substantial Communist Party in Britain and provided the country with a generous supply of men and women of sterling moral character from mainly working-class families. Its decline is a substantial part of the explosions both of unwanted motherhood and of crime in recent decades. There is also the tremendous determination shown by John Wesley in spending year after year riding for miles every day, preaching more than seven sermons a week, and so on. I have only recently been told of Wesley's great controversy against predestination and in favor of the Arminian alternative. Certainly he was one of my country's many great sons and daughters. One at least of the others was raised in a Methodist home with a father who was a local preacher.

Habermas: Don't you attribute some of your appreciation for the Wesleys to your father's ministry? Haven't you said that your father was the first non-Anglican to get a doctorate in theology from Oxford University?

Flew: Yes to both questions. Of course it was because my family's background was that of Methodism. Yes, my father was also president of the Methodist Conference for the usual single-year term, and he was the Methodist representative of one or two other organizations. He was also concerned for the World Council of Churches. Had my father lived to be active into the early 1970s, he would have wanted at least to consider the question of whether the Methodist Church ought not to withdraw from the World Council of Churches. That had by that time apparently been captured by agents of the USSR.[35]

Habermas: What do you think that Bertrand Russell, J. L. Mackie and A. J. Ayer would have thought about these theistic developments, had they still been alive today?

Flew: I think Russell certainly would have had to notice these things. I'm sure Mackie would have been interested too. I never knew Ayer very well, beyond meeting him once or twice.

Habermas: Do you think any of them would have been impressed in the direction of theism? I'm thinking here, for instance, about Russell's famous comments that God hasn't produced suffi-

---

[35]Bernard Smith, *The Fraudulent Gospel: Politics and the World Council of Churches* (London: Foreign Affairs, 1977).

cient evidence of his existence.[36]

Flew: Consistent with Russell's comments that you mention, Russell would have regarded these developments as evidence. I think we can be sure that Russell would have been impressed too, precisely because of his comments to which you refer. This would have produced an interesting second dialogue between him and that distinguished Catholic philosopher Frederick Copleston.

Habermas: In recent years you've been called the world's most influential philosophical atheist. Do you think Russell, Mackie or Ayer would have been bothered or even angered by your conversion to theism? Or do you think that they would have at least understood your reasons for changing your mind?

Flew: I'm not sure how much any of them knew about Aristotle. But I am almost certain that they never had in mind the idea of a God who was not the God of any revealed religion. But we can be sure that they would have examined these new scientific arguments.

Habermas: C. S. Lewis explained in his autobiography that he moved first from atheism to theism and only later from theism to Christianity. Given your great respect for Christianity, do you think that there is any chance that you might in the end move from theism to Christianity?

Flew: I think it's very unlikely, due to the problem of evil. But, if it did happen, I think it would be in some eccentric fit and doubtfully orthodox form: regular religious practice perhaps, but without belief. If I wanted any sort of future life I should become a Jehovah's Witness. But some things I am completely confident about. I would never regard Islam with anything but horror and fear because it is fundamentally committed to conquering the world for Islam. It was because the whole of Palestine was part of the Land of Islam that Muslim Arab armies moved in to try to destroy Israel at birth and why the struggle for the return of the still surviving refugees and their

---

[36]See, for example, Bertrand Russell, *Bertrand Russell Speaks His Mind*, ed. Woodrow Wyatt (New York: Bard Books, 1960), pp. 19-20.

numerous descendents continues to this day.

Habermas: I ask this last question with a smile, Tony. But just think what would happen if one day you were pleasantly disposed toward Christianity and all of a sudden the resurrection of Jesus looked pretty good to you?

Flew: Well, one thing I'll say in this comparison is that, for goodness' sake, Jesus is an enormously attractive charismatic figure, which the Prophet of Islam most emphatically is not.

Antony Flew's Deism Revisited

A Review Essay on *There Is a God*

Gary R. Habermas

> *There Is a God: How the World's Most Notorious Atheist Changed His Mind.* By Antony Flew and Roy Abraham Varghese. New York: HarperCollins, 2007. 256 pages. $24.95.

When preeminent philosophical atheist Antony Flew announced in 2004 that he had come to believe in God's existence and was probably best considered a Deist, the reaction from both believers and skeptics was "off the chart." Few religious stories had this sort of appeal and impact, across the spectrum, both popular as well as theoretical. No recent change of mind has received this much attention. Flew responded by protesting that his story really did not deserve this much interest. But as he explained repeatedly, he simply had to go where the evidence led.

SOME BACKGROUND

It was this last sentence, repeated often in interviews, that really interested me. Having known Tony well over twenty years, I had heard him repeat many things like it, as well as other comments that might be termed "open minded." He had insisted that he was open to God's existence, to special revelation, to miracles, to an afterlife or to David Hume being in error on this or that particular point. To be truthful, I tended to set aside his comments, thinking that, while they were made honestly, perhaps Tony still was not as open as he had thought.

Then very early in 2003 Tony indicated to me that he was considering theism, backing off a few weeks later and saying he remained an atheist with "big questions." One year later, in January 2004, Tony told me he had indeed become a theist, just as quickly adding, however, that he was "not the revelatory kind" of believer. That was when I heard him say for the first time that he was just following where the evidence led. Then I remembered all the earlier occasions when he had insisted that he was not objecting to God or the supernatural realm on a priori grounds. I was amazed. Tony was indeed willing to consider the evidence.

There was an immediate outcry from many in the skeptical community. Perhaps Tony Flew was simply too old or had not kept up on the relevant literature. The presumption seemed to be that, if he had been doing so, then he would not have experienced such a change of mind. One joke quipped that, at his advanced age, maybe he was just hedging his bets in favor of an afterlife.

One persistent rumor was that Tony Flew really did not believe in God after all. Or perhaps he had already recanted his mistake. Paul Kurtz's foreword to the republication of Flew's classic volume *God and Philosophy* identified me as "an evangelical Christian philosopher at Jerry Falwell's Liberty University," noting my interview with Flew and my "interpretation" that Tony now believed in God.[37] Kurtz seemed to think that perhaps the question still remained as to whether Flew believed in God. After explaining that Flew's "final introduction" to the reissued volume had undergone the process of four drafts, Kurtz concluded that readers should "decide whether or not he has abandoned his earlier views."[38]

In his introduction to this same text, Flew both raised at least a half-dozen new issues since his book had first appeared in 1966 and mentioned questions about each of these subjects. Included were discussions on contemporary cosmology, fine-tuning arguments, some thoughts regarding Darwin's work, reflections on Aristotle's

---

[37]Paul Kurtz, foreword to Antony Flew, *God and Philosophy* (Amherst, N.Y.: Prometheus, 2005), p. 6.
[38]Ibid., pp. 6-7.

view of God as well as Richard Swinburne's many volumes on God and Christian theism. Hints of theism were interspersed alongside some tough questions.[39]

Of course, book text must be completed well before the actual date of publication. But several news articles had appeared first, telling the story of what Flew referred to as his "conversion."[40] Early in 2005, my lengthy interview with Flew was published in *Philosophia Christi*.[41] Another excellent interview was conducted by Jim Beverly, in which Flew also evaluated the influence of several major Christian philosophers.[42]

In many of these venues, Flew explained in his own words that he was chiefly persuaded to abandon atheism because of Aristotle's writings about God and due to a number of arguments that are often associated with Intelligent Design. But his brand of theism—or better yet, Deism[43]—was not a variety that admitted special revelation, including either miracles or an afterlife. While he acknowledged most of the traditional attributes for God, he stopped short of affirming any divine involvement with humans.

Along the way, Flew made several very positive comments about Christianity, and about Jesus, in particular. Jesus was a first-rate moral philosopher, as well as a preeminent charismatic personality, while Paul had a brilliant philosophical mind. While rejecting mir-

---

[39]Flew, *God and Philosophy*, pp. 10-16.

[40]Examples include the Associated Press, "There Is a God, Leading Atheist Concludes," December 9, 2004; David Roach, "Famed Atheist Sees Evidence for God, Cites Recent Discoveries," *BP News*, December 13, 2004; David Roach, "Atheist's Turn Toward God Was a Four-Year Process, Friend Says," *BP News*, December 22, 2004; Gene Edward Veith, "Flew the Coup," *World Magazine*, 2004; mention was also made in columns such as "Quotables" and "The Buzz," both in *World Magazine*, 2004.

[41]Antony Flew and Gary Habermas, "My Pilgrimage from Atheism to Theism: A Discussion Between Antony Flew and Gary Habermas," *Philosophia Christi* 6 (2004): 197-211.

[42]James A. Beverly, "Thinking Straighter," *Christianity Today*, April 2005, pp. 80-83.

[43]In our discussion for *Philosophia Christi*, I asked Tony which term he preferred. He was convinced that *theism* was the better word for the article, even if less accurate, because he thought that the nuances of *Deism* were not well known and would raise too many definitional issues. But it turned out that *Deism* was well received, hence its more accurate use in this article.

acles, Flew held that the resurrection is the best-attested miracle claim in history.[44]

It is against this background that we turn to the latest chapter in the ongoing account of Antony Flew's pilgrimage from ardent atheism to Deism. Further clarifying his religious views, especially for those who might have thought that the initial report was too hasty, or suspected incorrect reporting, or later backtracking on Flew's part, the former atheistic philosopher has now elucidated his position. In a new book, Flew chronicles the entire story of his professional career, from atheism to Deism, including more specific reasons for his change. Along the way, several new aspects have been added.

ANTONY FLEW'S INFLUENCE

Signifying his change of view, the cover of Flew's new book cleverly reads, "There Is No God," but the word *No* is scribbled out and the word *A* is handwritten above it. Flew terms this work his "last will and testament," noting that the subtitle "was not my own invention."[45] The contents are nothing short of a treasure trove of details from Flew's life, including his family, education, publications and interactions with many now world-famous philosophers, not to mention the long-awaited reasons for his becoming a Deist.

The volume begins with a preface written by Roy Varghese,[46] followed by an introduction by Flew. Part one, "My Denial of the Divine," contains three chapters on Flew's previous atheism.

The book opens with a reverberating bang. Varghese's eighteen-page preface sets the tone for much of the remainder of the text. He begins with the breaking news in late 2004 of Antony Flew's newly

---

[44]For some details, see Flew and Habermas, "My Pilgrimage from Atheism to Theism," reprinted here.

[45]Antony Flew and Roy Abraham Varghese, *There Is a God: How the World's Most Notorious Atheist Changed His Mind* (New York: HarperCollins, 2007), p. 1.

[46]Varghese is a long-time philosophical and scientific conference organizer, editor and winner of a 1996 Templeton Book Prize for Outstanding Books in Science and Natural Theology.

announced belief in God. Varghese then notes that the response
to the Associated Press story from Flew's fellow atheists verged on
hysteria. . . . "Inane insults and juvenile caricatures were common
in the freethinking blogosphere. The same people who complained
about the Inquisition and witches being burned at the stake were
now enjoying a little heresy hunting of their own. The advocates
of tolerance were not themselves very tolerant. And, apparently, religious zealots don't have a monopoly on dogmatism, incivility, fa-
naticism, and paranoia."[47]

Varghese ends by stating, "Flew's position in the history of atheism transcends anything that today's atheists have on offer."[48]

This last comment serves as an entree to two of the more interesting arguments in the book. Considering Flew's impact in the history
of modern atheism, Varghese argues initially that "within the last
hundred years, no mainstream philosopher has developed the kind
of systematic, comprehensive, original, and influential exposition of
atheism that is to be found in Antony Flew's fifty years of anti-
theological writings."[49] He then considers the contributions to atheism produced by well-known philosophers such as A. J. Ayer, Bertrand Russell, Jean-Paul Sartre, Albert Camus and Martin Heidegger.
Varghese finds that none of these scholars "took the step of developing book-length arguments to support their personal beliefs."[50]

More recent writers are also mentioned, among them Richard
Rorty, Jacques Derrida, J. L. Mackie, Paul Kurtz and Michael Martin.
While they might be said to have contributed more material on behalf of atheism, "their works did not change the agenda and framework of discussion the way Flew's innovative publications did."[51]

But Flew's writings, such as "Theology and Falsification" ("the

---

[47]Flew, *There Is a God*, p. viii.
[48]Ibid.
[49]Ibid., p. ix.
[50]Ibid., p. x.
[51]Ibid.

most widely reprinted philosophical publication of the last century"[52]), *God and Philosophy, The Presumption of Atheism* and other publications, set the philosophical tone of atheism for a generation of scholars. Along with Flew's many other books and essays, one could hardly get through a contemporary philosophy class, especially in philosophy of religion, without being at least introduced to his theses.

Varghese also raises a second crucial topic in the history of twentieth-century philosophy—Flew's relation to logical positivism. Many works treat Flew's ideas, especially those in "Theology and Falsification," as a more subtle, analytic outgrowth of positivism. Sometimes it is thought that Flew attempted to refurbish a less dogmatic application of the discredited verification principle, popularized by Ayer's *Language, Truth, and Logic*.[53]

However, Flew did not interpret his essay in this manner. In 1990, he explained his thinking that logical positivism made an "arrogant announcement" that sought to rule out theology and ethics in an a priori manner. The resulting discussion had often become stagnated. Flew wanted to provide an opportunity for the free discussion of religious issues: "Let the believers speak for themselves, individually and severally."[54]

In an article in 2000, Flew explained that his purpose in first reading the paper at a meeting of C. S. Lewis's Socratic Club was that "I wanted to set these discussions off onto new and hopefully more fruitful lines."[55] In another interview that I did with Tony in Oxford in 2005, he attested that he saw his essay as slamming the door on positivism at the Socratic Club. He attests that his essay "was intended to simply refute the positivistic stance against reli-

---

[52]Ibid., p. 8.
[53]A. J. Ayer, *Language, Truth, and Logic* (New York: Dover, 1946). In the introduction to this later edition of the 1936 work, Ayer acknowledges that the assault on the verification principle succeeded in pointing out some flaws in the concept (pp. 5-26).
[54]Flew, *There Is a God*, p. xiv.
[55]Antony Flew, "Theology and Falsification: A Golden Jubilee Celebration," *Philosophy Now*, October/November 2000, p. 28.

gious utterances. It succeeded in that, but then its influence spread outside of Oxford."[56]

These two topics—Flew's influence on the philosophical atheism of the second half of the twentieth century and his purpose in first presenting his essay "Theology and Falsification"—are key chapters in the life of this major British philosopher. Varghese does well to remind us of Flew's influence. As he concludes, it is in this context that "Flew's recent rejection of atheism was clearly a historic event."[57]

Flew then begins the remainder of the book with an introduction. Referring to his "conversion" from atheism to Deism, he begins by affirming clearly that "I now believe there is a God!"[58] As for those detractors who blamed this on Flew's "advanced age" and spoke of a sort of "deathbed conversion," Flew reiterates what he has said all along: he still rejects the afterlife and is not placing any "Pascalian bets."[59]

In a couple of stunning comments, Flew then reminds his readers that he had changed his mind on other major issues throughout his career. He states, "I was once a Marxist." Then, more than twenty years ago, "I retracted my earlier view that all human choices are determined entirely by physical causes."[60]

THE MAKING OF AN ATHEIST

Part one ("My Denial of the Divine") consists of three chapters, intriguingly titled, "The Creation of an Atheist," "Where the Evidence Leads" and "Atheism Calmly Considered." This material is simply a delightful read, consisting of many autobiographical details regard-

---

[56]Antony Flew, "From Atheism to Deism: A Conversation Between Antony Flew and Gary Habermas," in *C. S. Lewis as Philosopher: Truth, Goodness and Beauty*, ed. Jerry L. Walls, David Baggett and Gary Habermas (Downers Grove, Ill.: IVP Academic, 2008).
[57]Flew, *There Is a God*, p. xi.
[58]Ibid., p. 1.
[59]Ibid., p. 2.
[60]Ibid., p. 3.

ing Flew's career and research, along with many enjoyable as well as amusing anecdotes.

In chapter one, Flew reviews his childhood and early life. This includes detailed references to his father: an Oxford University graduate with two years of study at Marburg University in Germany, who had become a Methodist minister very much interested in evangelism, as well as a professor of New Testament at a theological college in Cambridge. It was from his father that Tony learned, at an early age, the value of good research and of checking relevant sources before drawing conclusions.

Flew even stated in some of his atheist publications that he was never satisfied with the way he had become an atheist—here described as a process that was accomplished "much too quickly, much too easily, and for what later seemed to me the wrong reasons." Incredibly, he now reflects on his early theism that changed to atheism: "for nearly seventy years thereafter I never found grounds sufficient to warrant any fundamental reversal."[61] Nonetheless, it was an aspect of the problem of evil that affected Tony's conversion to atheism. During family travels to Germany, he witnessed firsthand some of the horrors of Nazi society and learned to detest "the twin evils of anti-Semitism and totalitarianism."[62]

Chapter one also includes accounts of Flew's basically private education at a boarding school, along with his years at Oxford University, interspersed with military service during World War II, as well as his "locking horns with C. S. Lewis" at Socratic Club meetings. He was present at the famous debate between Lewis and Elizabeth Anscombe in February 1948. Flew also met his wife, Annis, at Oxford. For all those (including myself) who have wondered through the years about Tony's incredible notions of ethical responsibility, he states that while he had left his father's faith, he retained his early

---

[61]This and the previous quote are from ibid., p. 13.
[62]Ibid., p. 14.

ethics, reflected in his treatment of Annis before their marriage.[63]

In chapter two, "Where the Evidence Leads," Flew reflects on his early tenure as "a hotly-energetic left-wing socialist,"[64] and narrates his early philosophical interests: parapsychology, Darwinian social ethics and the notion of evolutionary progress, problems with idealism, and analytic philosophy. More details on the Socratic Club introduce some of the philosophical reactions to Flew's "Theology and Falsification," along with his writing of his epic *God and Philosophy*, his "systematic argument for atheism."[65] Flew discusses reactions from Richard Swinburne, J. L. Mackie and Frederick Copleston. His conclusion today, as Tony has told me on several occasions, is that *God and Philosophy* is "a historical relic," due to changes in his thinking that arose from the response of others to his writing. These changes are set forth in this volume.

Flew also discusses in chapter two his well-known volumes *The Presumption of Atheism* and *Hume's Philosophy of Belief*. Philosophical reactions are recounted from Anthony Kenny, Kai Nielsen, Ralph McInerny and especially Alvin Plantinga, whose thoughts Flew calls, "By far, the headiest challenge to the argument" of the former volume.[66] The chapter concludes with Flew's changes of mind regarding some of Hume's ideas, plus his holding and then abandoning compatibilism.[67]

Ending his section on his atheism, Flew's third chapter is "Atheism Calmly Considered." Here he notes a number of his debates and dialogues over the years, both public and written, with Thomas Warren, William Lane Craig, Terry Miethe, Richard Swinburne, Richard Dawkins and myself. He also mentions two conferences. The first ("The Shootout at the O.K. Corral") in Dallas in 1985 featured four prominent atheistic philosophers, playfully called "gunslingers"

---

[63]Ibid., pp. 22-26.
[64]Ibid., p. 33.
[65]Ibid., p. 49.
[66]Ibid., p. 55.
[67]Ibid., pp. 56-64.

(Flew, Paul Kurtz, Wallace Matson and Kai Nielson), dueling with four equally prominent theistic philosophers (Alvin Plantinga, Ralph McInerny, George Mavrodes and William Alston). The second conference at New York University in 2004 notably included Scottish philosopher John Haldane and Israeli physicist Gerald Schroeder. Here Flew stunned the participants by announcing that he had come to believe in God.[68]

THERE IS A GOD

The second half of the book consists of the long-awaited reasons for Flew's conversion to Deism, titled "My Discovery of the Divine." It includes seven chapters on Flew's religious pilgrimage, along with the nature of the universe and life. Two appendices complete the volume.

"A Pilgrimage of Reason," chapter four, is the initial contribution to this section. In this essay, Flew chiefly makes the crucial point that his approach to God's existence has been philosophical, not scientific. As he notes, "My critics responded by triumphantly announcing that I had not read a particular paper in a scientific journal or followed a brand-new development relating to abiogenesis." But in so doing, "they missed the whole point." Flew's conversion was due to philosophical arguments, not scientific ones: "To think at this level is to think as a philosopher. And, at the risk of sounding immodest, I must say that this is properly the job of philosophers, not of the scientists as scientists."[69]

Thus, if scientists want to get into the fray, they "will have to stand on their own two philosophical feet."[70] Similarly, "a scientist who speaks as a philosopher will have to furnish a philosophical case. As Albert Einstein himself said, 'The man of science is a poor

---

[68]Ibid., p. 74.
[69]Ibid., p. 90.
[70]Ibid.

philosopher.'"[71] Flew ends the chapter by pointing out that it is Aristotle who most exemplifies his search: "I was persuaded above all by the philosopher David Conway's argument for God's existence" drawn from "the God of Aristotle."[72]

The fifth chapter, "Who Wrote the Laws of Nature?" discusses the views of many major scientists, including Einstein and Hawking, along with philosophers like Swinburne and Plantinga, to argue that there is a connection between the laws of nature and the "Mind of God."[73] Flew thinks that this is still a philosophical discussion. As Paul Davies asserted in his Templeton address, "science can proceed only if the scientist adopts an essentially theological worldview," because "even the most atheistic scientist accepts as an act of faith the existence of a lawlike order in nature that is at least in part comprehensible to us."[74] The existence of these laws must be explained. Flew concludes that many contemporary thinkers "propound a vision of reality that emerges from the conceptual heart of modern science and imposes itself on the rational mind. It is a vision that I personally find compelling and irrefutable."[75]

Chapter six, "Did the Universe Know We Were Coming?" discusses fine-tuning arguments and the multiverse option as another angle on the laws of nature. Among the opponents of the multiverse option, Flew lists Davies, Swinburne and himself, in part because it simply extends the questions of life and nature's laws.[76] Regardless, Flew concludes, "So multiverse or not, we still have to come to terms with the origins of the laws of nature. And the only viable explanation here is the divine Mind."[77]

Chapter seven, "How Did Life Go Live?" continues what Flew in-

---

[71]Ibid., p. 91.
[72]Ibid., p. 92.
[73]Ibid., p. 103.
[74]Ibid., p. 107.
[75]Ibid., p. 112.
[76]Ibid., pp. 118-19.
[77]Ibid., p. 121.

sists is a philosophical rather than a scientific discussion of items that are relevant to God's existence. He discusses at least three chief issues: how there can be fully materialistic explanations for the emergence of life, the problem of reproduction at the very beginning and DNA. Although science has not concluded its treatment of these matters either, they are answering questions that are different from the philosophical issues that Flew is addressing.[78] Flew concludes by agreeing with George Wald that "the only satisfactory explanation for the origin of such 'end-directed, self replicating' life as we see on earth is an infinitely intelligent Mind."[79]

In the title of chapter eight, Flew asks, "Did Something Come from Nothing?" In spite of our twenty years of friendship, I was still not prepared to see Tony developing and defending a cosmological argument for God's existence. In an essay published back in 1994, he had raised questions about David Hume's philosophy and its inability to explain causation or the laws of nature.[80] Then, works by philosophers David Conway and Richard Swinburne convinced him that Hume could be answered on the cosmological argument as well. Buoyed by these refutations of Hume, Flew was now free to explore the relation between a cosmological argument for God's existence and recent discussions regarding the beginning of the universe. Flew concludes that "Richard Swinburne's cosmological argument provides a very promising explanation, probably the finally right one."[81]

In chapter nine, "Finding Space for God," Flew begins with his longtime objection to God, that a concept of "an incorporeal omnipresent Spirit" is incoherent—something analogous to talking about a "person without a body."[82] But through the 1980s and 1990s, theistic philosophers in the analytic tradition enjoyed a renaissance. Two of these, Thomas Tracy and Brian Leftow (who succeeded Swinburne at

---

[78]Ibid., p. 129.
[79]Ibid., p. 132.
[80]Ibid., p. 139.
[81]Ibid., p. 145.
[82]Ibid., p. 148.

Oxford), answered Flew's questions. Flew now concedes that the concept of an omnipresent Spirit outside space and time is not intrinsically incoherent.[83]

In "Open to Omnipotence," chapter ten, Flew summarizes that his case for God's existence centers on three philosophical items: the origin of the laws of nature, the organization of life and the origin of life. What about the problem of evil? Flew states that this is a separate question, but he has two chief options: an Aristotelian God who does not interfere in the world or the free-will defense. He prefers the former, especially since he thinks the latter relies on special revelation.[84]

Closing the main portion of the book with some further shocking comments, Flew states, "I am entirely open to learning more about the divine Reality," including "whether the Divine has revealed itself in human history." The reason: everything but the logically impossible is "open to omnipotence."[85]

Further, "As I have said more than once, no other religion enjoys anything like the combination of a charismatic figure like Jesus and a first-class intellectual like St. Paul. If you're wanting omnipotence to set up a religion, it seems to me that this is the one to beat!"[86] He ends the chapter a few sentences later: "Some claim to have made contact with this Mind. I have not—yet. But who knows what could happen next? Some day I might hear a Voice that says, 'Can you hear me now?'"[87]

Two appendices close the book. The first is an evaluation of the "New Atheism" of writers like Richard Dawkins, Daniel Dennett and Sam Harris. The author of the first appendix, Roy Varghese, argues that "five phenomena are evident in our immediate experience that can only be explained in terms of the existence of God."[88] These five

---

[83]Ibid., pp. 153-54.
[84]Ibid., p. 156.
[85]Ibid., pp. 156-57.
[86]Ibid., p. 157; see also pp. 185-86.
[87]Ibid., p. 158.
[88]Ibid., p. 161.

are rationality, life, consciousness, conceptual thought and the human self, each of which he discusses. Varghese concludes that by arguing from "everyday experience" we are able to "become immediately aware that the world of living, conscious, thinking beings has to originate in a living Source, a Mind."[89]

The second appendix is an essay on the self-revelation of God, written by New Testament theologian N. T. Wright, with brief responses by Flew. Wright argues very succinctly that Jesus existed, was God incarnate and rose from the dead.[90] Flew precedes this treatment by commenting that though he does not believe the miracle of the resurrection, it "is more impressive than any by the religious competition."[91] Flew's final reflection on Wright's material is that it is an impressive argument—"absolutely wonderful, absolutely radical, and very powerful." In the end, Flew remains open to divine revelation, since omnipotence could act in such a manner.[92]

COMMENTS

As I have indicated, Flew's new book is a delightful read. This especially applies to the many autobiographical details. The intersection of his life with some of the best-known philosophers in the previous half-century was nothing short of exhilarating.

It will be no surprise to anyone who has followed my published debates or dialogues with Tony that the clarification found in this volume was more than welcome. For one thing, many of his comments here were also made in our published dialogue in *Philosophia Christi*. Most of all, this book should clear up the rumors as to the nature of Tony's "conversion." He indeed believes in God, and while from the beginning rejecting special revelation along with any religious affiliation, his view of God's nature is otherwise quite robust.

---

[89]Ibid., p. 183.
[90]Ibid., pp. 187-213.
[91]Ibid., p. 187.
[92]Ibid., p. 213.

Indeed, his Deism includes most of the classical theological attributes. Further, Flew is clear several times that he is open to special revelation. As he told me just recently, he "won't shut the door" to the possibility of such revelation or even to hearing a word from the Deity.[93]

Of course, I predict that various skeptics will still have profound problems with the book's content. They will not be satisfied with its proclamations. I can only imagine the nature of the complaints. If I am right about this, it may even confirm further Varghese's charge of the vociferous nature of this community's response to the original announcement. If Varghese is also correct that Flew had produced the most vigorous defense of philosophical atheism in the last century, a guess is that some skeptics are still stung by the loss of their most prominent philosophical supporter.

I would like to have seen further clarification on a few issues in the book. For instance, it would have been very helpful if Tony had explained the precise sense in which he thought that "Theology and Falsification" was an attempt to curtail the growth of positivism. That has remained unclear to me. I too was taught that the article was a defense of an analytic position that only softened the force of the positivistic challenge.

Another potential question surrounds Tony's excellent distinction between giving philosophical as opposed to scientific reasons for his belief in God. However, a discussion or chart that maps out the differences between the two methodological stances would have been very helpful. Philosophers are used to these distinctions. But I am sure that others will think that Tony is still providing two sorts of arguments for God: Aristotle plus *scientific* arguments like Intelligent Design scenarios.

As Tony has said several times in recent years, he remains open to the possibility of special revelation, miracles like Jesus' resurrection, and the afterlife. In this volume he also continues to be very compli-

---

[93]Antony Flew in discussion with the author, October 3, 2007.

mentary toward these options. I cannot pursue further this topic here. While he mentioned evil and suffering, I did wonder about Tony's juxtaposition of choosing either Aristotle's Deism or the free-will defense, which he thinks "depends on the prior acceptance of a framework of divine revelation."[94] It seems to me that the free-will defense neither asks nor requires any such revelatory commitment. So I think that it could be pursued by a Deist too. If so, that is one more potential defeater to the evil and suffering issue. I will leave it here for now.

---

[94]Flew, *There Is a God*, p. 156.

PART III

Resurrection Matters
Assessing the Habermas/Flew Discussion

David Baggett

HABERMAS AND FLEW HAVE DONE us all a service by taking the time and effort to dialogue on this issue of the resurrection of Jesus. Few questions could be more important than this one. If Jesus didn't literally rise from the dead, then at most we would have to settle for a demythologized and deflationary analysis of Christianity. The fact is, classical Christianity would be false, and Jesus likely a philosopher at best or a madman at worst. If Jesus did bodily rise from the grave, what could be more important as a clue to the meaning of life? The resurrection matters.

Flew and Habermas have now debated three times. This third debate was likely their last. With all three of their dialogues now in print, it's a good time to step back and provide a bit of analysis and perspective. The last couple of decades have seen a resurgence of interest in historical and evidential arguments for the truth of Christianity. Even Reformed epistemologist Alvin Plantinga, usually pessimistic in his assessments of such arguments, has acknowledged that scholars like F. F. Bruce, William Lane Craig, Stephen T. Davis, Gary Habermas and N. T. Wright have "produced serious and sometimes impressive historical arguments." Despite some of his former criticisms of evidentialism, he's made it clear it wasn't his intention to "denigrate their excellent work, or suggest that it isn't worthy of serious consideration."[1]

So in this chapter I propose we quickly review the evidence on which Habermas bases his argument, review criticisms of it, then assess those objections. Then we can move to the inference Habermas makes and criticisms of it, and then look at various philosophical questions the debate has raised. Finally, we will return to Flew and discuss not only where he is now in his fascinating intellectual journey but where he may be headed next.

THE HISTORICAL EVIDENCE

Habermas is wont to say that if biblical inerrancy is true, his case for resurrection will go through. That is obvious. More interestingly, he contends that it will also go through if biblical inerrancy is false. Habermas doesn't construct his case on subjective feelings, private conviction, personal faith, religious dogma or even any particular claim about the authority of the Bible. He builds his argument on evidence—"minimal facts" as he puts it—accepted as fact by the vast majority of critical scholars, irrespective of where they come down on the theological spectrum, from archconservative to ultraliberal or anywhere in between. He doesn't cherry pick scholars on the basis of personal preferences, but gleans the best historical research and nearly unanimous scholarly judgments established by early, multiple and eyewitness accounts. Compelling and corroborating historically grounded reasons from a variety of angles confirm each piece of the foundation on which he builds. When a piece of evidence is very controversial, like Mark 16:9-20, which isn't in the two earliest manuscripts, he simply does not include it in his case.

The resurrection conclusion Habermas wants to defend is that Jesus, having been dead, became alive again. Expressed like this, note the way it's a rather standard-sounding, empirically testable claim.

---

[1]Alvin Plantinga, "Historical Arguments and Dwindling Probabilities: A Response to Timothy McGrew," *Philosophia Christi* 8, no. 1 (2006): 19-20.

That it implies an ambitious claim philosophically or metaphysically doesn't detract from the fact that the claim is, in one sense, an historical one that is testable like any other. The uniqueness and philosophical implications of the claim will be taken up later, but Habermas would prefer to keep the historical debate, initially at least, confined to the claim that Jesus was alive (subsequent to death by crucifixion). There are advantages to doing this, as we will see, but it puts more of an evidential onus on the additional inferences required to arrive at the full range of Christian theological teaching. It also invites the criticism that it underplays the miraculous nature of the claim, but we will put off a discussion of this until later, including the powerful rejoinder that it better enables the historian as historian to assess it.

The number of "minimal facts" is arguably arbitrary, but Habermas often adduces these twelve, as listed earlier:

1. Jesus died by crucifixion.

2. He was buried.

3. The death of Jesus caused the disciples to despair and lose hope, believing that his life was ended.

4. Although not as widely accepted, many scholars hold that the tomb in which Jesus was buried was discovered to be empty just a few days later.

5. The disciples had experiences they believed were the literal appearances of the risen Jesus.

6. The disciples were transformed from doubters who were afraid to identify themselves with Jesus to bold proclaimers of his death and resurrection.

7. This message was the center of preaching in the early church.

8. This message was especially proclaimed in Jerusalem, where Jesus died and was buried shortly before.

9. As a result of this teaching, the church was born and grew.

10. Sunday became the primary day of worship.

11. James, who had been a skeptic, was converted to the faith when he also believed that he had seen the resurrected Jesus.

12. A few years later, Paul was converted by an experience that he likewise believed to be an appearance of the risen Jesus.[2]

Habermas's procedure here echoes that of other scholars. William Lane Craig typically constructs his historical case for the resurrection on four facts: Jesus' burial, the discovery of his empty tomb, his postmortem appearances and the origin of the disciples' belief in his resurrection. Other scholars, from N. T. Wright to Robert Funk to E. P. Sanders to Luke Timothy Johnson to Geza Vermes, start with lists of their own. It's a common method because the historical evidence for such a set of groundwork facts is very strong. Habermas also offers a "core-facts" case that's more minimalist and doesn't require the use of the Gospels but is still arguably adequate for certain purposes. It contains just four to seven facts, none of which is disputed by many scholars: Jesus' death by crucifixion, the subsequent experiences that the disciples were convinced were literal appearances of the risen Jesus, the corresponding transformation of these men and Paul's conversion experience after what he believed to be an appearance of the risen Jesus.

We won't reiterate in detail all the various evidences for each fact Habermas cites, but evidence is a vital part of his case. My philosopher friends often tend to be the most skeptical of the resurrection argument, sometimes even before hearing the evidence on which it's based. Perhaps part of the reason for this is that this argument is rooted in history. It has an obstinate concreteness to it that abstract arguments from natural theology don't have. Philosophers tend to prefer abstract evidence, for some reason, and I mention this because

---

[2]See Gary R. Habermas, *The Historical Jesus: Ancient Evidence for the Life of Christ* (Joplin, Mo.: College Press, 1996), p. 158.

I'm one of them. But Christianity is historically rooted, and its truth is wholly dependent on the fact that a literal bodily resurrection really happened. So if we're going to consider the evidence for Christianity, there's simply no way around this, and thinkers whose affinity for the abstract disinclines them from such historical arguments from the start need to recognize this personal preference for what it is. There are indeed hugely important philosophical questions that the argument raises, but a vital aspect of the case is historical, and judgments about it should be evidential in nature, not preformed philosophical judgments or dogmatic pronouncements that serve as an excuse from considering the evidence closely.

I once proposed the resurrection argument to an atheist friend who had been a philosophy professor for many years, referring to the consensus among critical scholars about Jesus' death by crucifixion. He responded incredulously that there are some scholars who deny that Jesus even lived. "Is it just a matter of picking whatever scholars say what we want to believe?" he asked. This response is as uninformed as it is unhelpful, because not all questions are historically up for grabs here. Are there scholars who deny that Jesus lived? Yes, and they are few and far out of the mainstream because their cases are so deficient in evidence. Habermas and Flew show the way that open and cordial dialogue ought to go. It's a real discussion and debate between philosophers interested in the truth, not just modern-day sophists interested in winning an argument, engaging in one-upmanship or doing whatever is necessary to arrive at a friendly conclusion or to avoid an unfriendly one.[3]

None of the facts Habermas adduces would deductively prove

---

[3]This anecdote also accentuates an interesting rhetorical disadvantage faced by defenders of the historical argument for the resurrection. Objections meant to cast doubt or to muddy the waters can often be expressed succinctly in a sentence or two. The response, which is usually devastating, might take thirty pages of reasoned and learned analysis, more than enough to exhaust the patience of most listeners. In a sound-bite culture like ours, this gives the skeptics a kind of strategic advantage, but one that's more appearance than reality. Thanks to Tim McGrew for this insight, shared in personal conversation (phone conversation, July 2008).

theism or Christianity to be true. Nor does accepting them require one to be sympathetic to Christianity or theism. The minimal facts are garden-variety historical claims. Unless any skepticism about them is grounded in evidence, it lacks credibility and doesn't advance the discussion. Substantial evidence supports each of the minimal facts. Merely scoffing at the evidence, writing it off as unknowable, casting doubt because, after all, that was a long time ago, pointing to lack of complete consensus among scholars, referring vaguely to a fuzzy epistemic situation surrounding such alleged facts or merely asserting that the evidence is deficient—none of these approaches carries the weight of rational conviction. And none serves as a substitute for honest examination of the actual evidence.

Skeptics remain, though, and raise various concerns, some of which we've seen in this debate between Flew and Habermas. So let's take a look at three kinds of concerns often raised, and offer a quick assessment of each. The three concerns are biblical and historical questions, certain undercutting defeaters and an analogical rebuttal. We'll consider each in turn.

Biblical and historical objections. There are three types of these: textual, temporal and contextual. *Textual concerns* pertain to the differing accounts of the resurrection events we find in various sources. Flew makes much of the differences between Paul's account and those of the Gospels. Bart Ehrman makes much of the disparities between the Gospels themselves.[4] Gerd Lüdemann casts doubt on the Gospel accounts because of their inconsistencies with the Gnostic Gospels.

Temporal concerns include uncertainty regarding something as basic as the birth of Jesus, the gap of time that elapses between the events in question and a written account of them and later accre-

---

[4]See "Is There Historical Evidence for the Resurrection of Jesus? A Debate Between William Lane Craig and Bart D. Ehrman," held at the College of the Holy Cross, Worcester, Mass., March 28, 2006, a transcript of which can be found at <www.holycross.edu/departments/crec/website/resurrdebate.htm>.

tions sometimes thought to have been added to augment the original documents.

Contextual concerns include the observation that resurrection stories were common among the mystery religions in that day and cultural milieu. Consequently, some claim it's not surprising that one more resurrection story would take hold and generate a following. The stronger the case for the resurrection, moreover, the harder it is to make sense of the relatively few initial followers of Christianity. Why weren't there more converts and more skeptics convinced? And isn't it likely that, in the transition from the Aramaic-speaking, Jerusalem-centered, Semitic context of the earliest Christians to the Greek-speaking, broader Hellenistic context of the New Testament several decades later, various legends would have grown and stories stretched in an effort to proliferate the faith and attract new converts?

Response to biblical and historical objections. Let's say a word about each of these, in reverse order. As to the suggestion that Christian resurrection stories merely echo the dying–rising god legends predating Christianity, from the Egyptian Osiris myth to the Norse Balder myth, a few points are in order. First, there are several reasons to think the Christian resurrection story didn't derive from earlier resurrection myths, not least because scholars now realize that there was very little influence from the mystery religions in first-century Palestine. There are also a number of obvious dissimilarities, such as this one: the gods in the mystery religions weren't historical persons, unlike Jesus. Most importantly, the Christian narrative is attributable to eyewitness accounts, clearly not the result of a borrowed legendary tradition. That there were these traditional myths predating Christianity scattered throughout the world vexed C. S. Lewis prior to his conversion, until he realized, with the help of J. R. R. Tolkien, that Christianity could be the "true myth." Here's how he put it in "Myth Became Fact":

The heart of Christianity is a myth which is also a fact. The old myth of the Dying God, *without ceasing to be myth*, comes down from the heaven of legend and imagination to the earth of history. It *happens*—at a particular date, in a particular place, followed by definable historical consequences. We pass from a Balder or an Osiris, dying nobody knows when or where, to a historical Person crucified (it is all in order) *under Pontius Pilate*. By becoming fact it does not cease to be myth: that is the miracle. I suspect that men have sometimes derived more spiritual sustenance from myths they did not believe than from the religion they professed. To be truly Christian we must both assent to the historical fact and also receive the myth (fact though it has become) with the same imaginative embrace which we accord to all myths. The one is hardly more necessary than the other.

If God chooses to be mythopoeic—and is not the sky itself a myth—shall we refuse to be mythopathic? For this is the marriage of heaven and earth: Perfect Myth and Perfect Fact: claiming not only our love and our obedience, but also our wonder and delight, addressed to the savage, the child, and the poet in each one of us no less than to the moralist, the scholar, and the philosopher.[5]

As to the number of converts and the question of why there weren't more of them if the resurrection really happened, the fact is that we're not told how many converts there were—though in Acts 2–3 a couple of large numbers are cited. But since we don't know the precise figures, this is an argument from silence, an argument predicated on what we don't know. Habermas contends that we should base our arguments here on what evidence we *do* have, not on evidence we *don't* have.

In terms of the cultural transition from the resurrection events to the New Testament, here are a few points: One of the most important

---

[5]C. S. Lewis, "Myth Became Fact," in *God in the Dock*, ed. Walter Hooper (Grand Rapids: Eerdmans, 1970), p. 67.

ways of establishing many of the minimal facts is 1 Corinthians 15:3 and following, in which Paul, very early on (A.D. 55 to 57), refers to the material he had received from others and passed on to others. The consensus among scholars is that Paul received this material from Peter and James on his first trip to Jerusalem. It predates Paul and is in the form of an early creed, evidence for which are the technical rabbinic words for passing on tradition, the stylized content, the proper names of Cephas (Peter's name in Aramaic, a reason to think the creed had an Aramaic origin) and James, and the non-Pauline locutions.

Paul had gone to Jerusalem to confirm that the message he himself had been proclaiming was the same message proclaimed there. Paul, whom Flew describes as having a first-rate philosophical mind, received this material, which confirms Jesus' appearances to various eyewitnesses, directly from some of those eyewitnesses. At the very least, he was able to confirm the appearances with eyewitnesses, which is exactly what we're told he did. Now here is the most interesting part of all, and this is unprecedented in the ancient world, where sources a couple hundred years after an event are often the best we have: Paul received this creed about three to eight years after the death of Jesus. The creed had been formulated before that, and the facts on which it was based yet earlier, which puts this report about the death and resurrection appearances of Jesus in the immediate aftermath of the events in question. For the historian, this sort of evidence is nothing less than golden.

What we too easily can underestimate today is the power of the oral tradition in that culture to keep the core message clear and on track. There are indeed some differences between that culture and ours, but this difference—the ability of that culture's oral traditions to keep the core message of the resurrection account straight until the written record was created—serves to strengthen the case that the message wasn't compromised or corrupted, especially since it was a message promulgated from the earliest days of the church, starting in the immediate aftermath of the resurrection. The early, multiple and eyewitness accounts form a constellation of corroborating evidence that helps answer the *temporal* concerns mentioned before.

Another difference between first-century Palestinian culture and ours helps answer one of the *textual* concerns expressed earlier. Recall that Ehrman noted how reading the Gospels horizontally raises a slew of problems about the accuracy of the biblical record. At least part of the answer to him is that, as New Testament scholar David Bauer puts it,

> The ancient understanding of history, which is shared by the biblical writers and their original audiences, is that history is not reducible to brute or nude fact, but is rather interpreted event, i.e., the deeper significance of the event is expressed in the way the event is described. This means that certain aspects of an event may be modified in the telling of it. This phenomenon accounts in large measure for the differences between the synoptic and Johannine tradition in the narrating of the same events. Bart Ehrman remains a fundamentalist epistemologically, reflecting the biases of modernity, in that he insists that if (ancient) writers do not measure up to the positivistic standards of Enlightenment historiography they must be repudiated.[6]

Readers today naturally wish to ask if this freedom that the ancient writers felt in conforming historical details to their intended narratives might have applied to events themselves, like the resurrection. But this overlooks the fact that none of the superficial, apparent discrepancies across the Gospels does anything to detract from the clear consensus on the central fact of the resurrection itself. The details are clearly peripheral to the central story. Failure to see that isn't tough-minded skepticism, but bad historiography.

Turning to the alleged differences between Paul's vision of Jesus and that of the disciples, I won't reiterate the compelling case Haber-

---

[6]Personal correspondence, June 20, 2008.

mas makes in this debate debunking those. When we consider the Gnostic Gospels, however, it's worth noting that some, like Gerd Lüdemann, think it instructive that there are various and relevant dissimilarities between the biblical accounts of the death and resurrection and those of the Gnostic Gospel accounts, differences that cast doubt on the biblical record. Robert Gundry's reply to Lüdemann on this point is worth repeating and is more than an adequate reply:

> Does Lüdemann expect us to believe that a Gnostic denial of Christ's death originated in Jerusalem, right where the crucifixion had taken place, right after Christ had died, so that burial was mentioned to counteract the denial? For lack of evidence there is not an ounce of scholarly consensus that a Gnostic denial of Christ's death had arisen by that time in that place. The very suggestion that it had would likely be greeted with guffaws among scholars, whatever their position on the resurrection. And to save his argument that the mention of burial in this earliest possible tradition coming out of Jerusalem aims to prove the reality of Christ's death, Lüdemann cannot take refuge in a supposedly Gnostic problem at Corinth two decades or so later, when Paul was writing 1 Corinthians.[7]

Undercutting defeaters objection. These are among the questions that David Hume famously raised in his writings about miracles. They don't directly demonstrate that the resurrection didn't happen, but rather that we have reasons for doubting some of the most important pieces of evidence that it did.

For example, take the people on whose testimony we're relying. We can, but need not, impugn their character by suggesting that at least some among them were lying; Flew is always careful to avoid doing this. Nonetheless, intellectual honesty demands certain recog-

---

[7]William Lane Craig and Gerd Lüdemann, *Jesus' Resurrection: Fact or Figment? A Debate Between William Lane Craig and Gerd Lüdemann*, ed. Paul Copan and Ronald K. Tacelli (Downers Grove, Ill.: InterVarsity Press, 2000), p. 119.

nitions, such as that these people lived in a very different time and place, where plausibility structures quite different from our own reigned. They may or may not have been "barbarous," to use Hume's term, but they were for the most part illiterate and uneducated, credulous and gullible, and filled with an intense need to hope for a better day of deliverance and salvation. Many of them were prone to ecstatic utterances, demon possessions were everyday realities, and claims to have witnessed divine visitations or miraculous occurrences undoubtedly carried with them a certain subcultural cachet. These people may well have been sincere, but may have been sincerely mistaken. What we know about religious psychology and superstition casts legitimate doubt over these stories. The possibility of honest error shows that the Lord, Liar, Lunatic hypotheses can too easily fail to exhaust alternatives.

Response to undercutting defeaters. Those on whose witness we're relying could have been sincere, but still wrong, even if not culpably so. Weren't the preponderance of those who claimed to see Jesus uneducated, ignorant, primitive, credulous people subject to radical confusion?

Put this starkly, one obvious reply is that this seems to overstate the case quite a bit, smacking of what C. S. Lewis once called chronological snobbery. Surely they weren't credulous about everything; they knew what death meant and that, say, people who were dead didn't get back up and start walking around. And they knew that someone slumped in the low position on the cross for a long time and no longer breathing meant death. Paul was clearly not an uneducated individual. He was highly trained, and Flew has repeatedly stressed that his was a top-notch philosophical mind. Numerous reports suggest that the disciples tended to be altogether skeptical when first hearing the news of Jesus' resurrection. In Paul's case, along with James's, we have complete skeptics, to whom something then happened to convince them that Jesus had indeed risen from the dead.

Analogical rebuttal objection. Miraculous accounts are ubiquitous across various religions around the world and throughout history. The vast majority of these alleged miracles are handily dismissed with the greatest of ease. Isn't it likely that the New Testament accounts of miracles are just as worthy of rejection? Are we to believe that, after the resurrection of Jesus, darkness covered the earth and earthquakes shook the world? Similar suspicions pervade most of our minds—and rightly so, many claim—when we hear other allegedly miraculous accounts like Muhammad's ascending to heaven on a horse, supposedly witnessed by five hundred, Joseph Smith's angelic visitation or visitations by Mary.

Response to analogical objection. Even though Habermas's initial resurrection conclusion is meant to be expressed in as nonmiraculous terms as possible, let's go ahead and discuss the analogical objection that keys in on this aspect of his eventual case. Since we typically consider ourselves entirely justified to be quite skeptical about miracle claims, why not so in this case too? If we're to believe that Jesus appeared to five hundred, why not believe, as legend has it, that Muhammad ascended to heaven on a white horse and was witnessed by hundreds as well? If we're to believe that Jesus appeared to the disciples, why not believe that Mary appeared to people at Fatima or Medjugorje? If we're instead going to remain skeptical about the latter cases, why not the former as well?

This is a fair question, but it seems to admit of a clear answer. Not every miracle claim is equal in evidential support. A prior decision to remain skeptical about all miracle claims, no matter what and come what may, because we're justifiably skeptical about some or most miracle reports, results in a refusal to consider the evidence. But as Habermas said in his first debate with Flew, scoffing at evidence is not the same as refuting it.

The story about Muhammad's ascension was a legend that grew up around him centuries afterward; there's simply no comparison in evidential support between that account and what evidence suggests followers of Jesus believed in the immediate aftermath of the resurrection. The vast majority of pilgrims to Fatima or Medjugorje see nothing, and those who do are likely to be witnessing an optical illusion of sorts (not a group hallucination) in light of the absence of objective corroboration.

The multiple, eyewitness and early reports of the resurrection of Jesus put this alleged miracle into an entirely different category. What seems irrefutable is that a great many people were completely convinced they had seen the risen Jesus. This doesn't prove a thing yet, granted, but the fact that their sincerity is well nigh beyond reproach—sincerity that led many of them to die for this belief— radically distinguishes their credibility from, say, that of Joseph Smith, the founder of Mormonism, as William Lane Craig explains:

> It's interesting that Smith and his father, when they lived in New York, were obsessed with finding Captain Kidd's buried gold. Then what does Smith later claim he finds? Golden plates from the Angel Moroni, and then they disappear and are supposedly taken to heaven and never seen again. What you have here is an elaborate hoax, compared to the gospels, with the evident sincerity of the people in what they were reporting. The problem with Mormonism is basically one of credibility because of the unreliability of Joseph Smith and a blatant lack of corroboration. Unlike the gospels, whose credibility has been greatly enhanced by archaeology, archaeological discoveries have repeatedly failed to substantiate the Book of Mormon.[8]

Biblical reports of earthquakes and darkness after the death of Jesus do admittedly seem farfetched, which reminds us that, in general, an attitude of skepticism is a good thing. But three points are in order. First, we should direct our skepticism not just toward miracle reports, but also toward an attitude that's categorically dismissive of miracles even when the evidence for them is strong. Second, there is, interestingly, some extrabiblical evidence to suggest that some such

---

[8]Lee Strobel, *The Case for Faith* (Grand Rapids: Zondervan, 2000), p. 71.

strange events were real. Thallus mentioned them in A.D. 52, for example. But third, and most importantly, nothing for present purposes—none of Habermas's minimal facts—rides on those earthquakes or that darkness being actual or on any particular analysis of that smattering of verses.

Conclusion. The early, independent and eyewitness testimony; the power of the oral tradition in that culture to preserve the core message of the resurrection event; the unprecedented number of corroborating documents that have enabled us to weed out the accretions and know with practical certainty what the original biblical record said about core doctrine and history—all of these pieces of evidence cast serious doubt on the skeptical challenges posed against the evidence on which Habermas constructs his case for the resurrection. Rather than weakening our confidence in the minimal facts, the questions should serve to bolster it. More could be said by way of defending these facts, but for now let's leave this question behind, tentatively proceeding on the assumption that we can assume these facts have been adequately established.

Nothing yet follows by way of theistic or miraculous conclusions. All we've done so far is look at the evidence and the historical case for it. As far as establishing these facts of history, Habermas's case is strong, built on solid principles of historical research. For example, take his first three core facts: Jesus' death by crucifixion, the subsequent experiences that the disciples were convinced of literal appearances of the risen Jesus and the corresponding transformation of these men. Considered respectively, it's no wonder that even Jesus Seminar cofounder John Dominic Crossan called the first fact the best established fact in ancient history; or that the similarly liberal biblical scholar Gerd Lüdemann says, "It may be taken as historically certain that Peter and the disciples had experiences after Jesus' death in which Jesus appeared to them as the risen Christ"[9]; or that

---

[9]Gerd Lüdemann, *What Really Happened to Jesus?* trans. John Bowden (Louisville, Ky.: Westminster John Knox Press, 1995), p. 8.

Luke Timothy Johnson, a New Testament scholar at Emory University, muses, "Some sort of powerful, transformative experience is required to generate the sort of movement earliest Christianity was."[10]

We ought to feel the force of this evidence. Take, for example, the willingness of the witnesses to the resurrection to die for their convictions. We are all familiar with plenty of zealous supporters of various causes, religious or political, willing to die for their beliefs. But this doesn't begin to approach what we have with the early followers of Jesus. They were willing to die over an empirical claim, having insisted that they had seen Jesus alive after he had died by brutal execution. They pointed to many infallible proofs and were willing to endure martyrdom over their eyewitness testimony. No cavalier mention of other proponents of worldviews or politics passionately but abstractly believed begins to compare with the power of this testimony. Affirming that the disciples were sincere in their belief requires no epistemic charity; the evidence for it is so overwhelming that to deny it is rationally indefensible.

Legitimate skeptical challenges are important to consider. We can hardly know without investigation whether the evidence is there or not. The challenges, however, fail to cast serious doubt on it. The operative question is whether this evidence is adequate to allow us rightly to infer the historicity of the resurrection. It's to this vitally important question we now turn.

THE RESURRECTION INFERENCE

Again, then, the inference that Habermas wishes to make is that the resurrection happened: Jesus had been dead, and later he was alive. If Jesus was dead by Friday afternoon and the next week was seen walking around then the resurrection happened. Whether he was raised by God or not, or raised with a body that was indestructible or not, are different matters. For now Habermas sets them aside, as he

---

[10]Luke Timothy Johnson, *The Real Jesus* (San Francisco: HarperSanFrancisco, 1996), p. 136.

also holds in abeyance further theological implications of the resurrection bearing on the overall truth of Christianity. The first question to answer is whether we can historically establish good reason to believe that Jesus came back to life.

Habermas often characterizes the nature of his inference as inductive, but he's also liable to explicate it in abductive terms, so that's what I'll do here. Abduction, or an "inference to the best explanation," is a common inference pattern found in fields of inquiry ranging from philosophy to science to history. Abductive inferences have a particular structure to them, which goes as follows: We come across some state of affairs or data in need of explanation. In this case the data will be Habermas's dozen minimal facts, all of which must be explained, not just some. We then compile a list of explanation candidates from which we will eventually choose. The five criteria by which we select the best explanation from among this pool are these: (a) explanatory power, (b) explanatory scope, (c) plausibility, (d) degree of "ad hoc–ness" and (e) conformity with other beliefs. The more explanatory power and scope and the more plausibility and conformity with other beliefs an explanation has, the better it is. The less ad hoc (adjusted, contrived, artificial) the explanation, the better as well. The trick is to subject all explanation options to these tests in order to pick the one that's the best—and therefore most likely true—explanation.

In the history of literature on the resurrection—from Albert Schweitzer to N. T. Wright to James Dunn to David Strauss to Wolfhart Pannenberg to Hans von Campenhausen to Rudolf Bultmann—a half-dozen explanation candidates have come to the fore in various formulations and combinations. They are (1) swoon theory, (2) fraud or stolen body theory, (3) hallucinations, (4) objective visions, (5) legend or myth theory, and (6) resurrection. So what we now need to do is apply the criteria for abduction to these explanation candidates to see which among them best explains the minimal facts.

With the possible exception of objective visions, and obviously the resurrection, all of these explanations are naturalistic. It's reasonable to give serious consideration first to naturalistic theories, if for no other reason than because miracles are by definition relatively rare. They are the exception, not the rule. Miracles, even if they're possible, shouldn't be our first guess. On this I agree with many of my secular friends; there's nothing wrong, and a lot right, with healthy skepticism. The abductive case to be made is only as strong as its weakest part. So let's look at the first five explanations and see how they fare, and we will keep this brief since this is largely a reiteration of key themes from the debate.

The swoon theory says Jesus didn't really die, but merely swooned, fainted, then came to, perhaps in the tomb, and walked away. When Flew in this last debate asked about evidence for an inhabited tomb, he was intimating that Jesus may not have died after all, despite evidence he was crucified. This is why Habermas spent time dwelling on the medical evidence of death. David Strauss is generally considered to have dispatched swoon theory long ago by the historical case against it.[11] The conviction of the disciples that they witnessed a gloriously resurrected Jesus, rather than a bleeding, horribly wounded man, makes it little wonder that the swoon theory was nearly universally abandoned long ago by all critical scholars in this area. The theory is weak both in terms of explanatory scope and power and in its implausibility in the light of what we know about crucifixions.

The fraud or stolen body theory says that the disciples lied and took the body themselves or it was stolen by others. Had the disciples done it, though, we would be hard pressed to explain their devotion to the cause and willingness to die, often quite horribly, for what they knew was a lie. The theory would thus be conspicuously lacking in explanatory power. Had others done it, what accounts for the appearances, and why wouldn't they produce the body to refute the resurrection? This theory lacks explanatory scope.

---

[11]David Strauss, *A New Life of Jesus*, 2nd ed. (Edinburgh: Williams and Norgate, 1879), 1:412.

Hallucinations of various sorts have been proposed to explain resurrection appearances, from grief-related hallucinations to guilt-induced hallucinations to conversion disorders. In all three debates between Flew and Habermas, Flew has expressed some openness to this idea as the likely explanation of resurrection appearances. Hallucinations lack explanatory scope, however, because they offer no explanation of the empty tomb. Nor do they explain why the disciples specifically believed in resurrection rather than in a vision of some sort. Hallucinations also lack explanatory power and plausibility because the appearances happened to believers and unbelievers (Paul and James), individuals and groups. Hallucinations don't happen in groups, moreover, despite claims to the contrary because of alleged visitations by Mary at, say, Fatima: the vast majority of people there don't claim to see anything. This was not the case with the resurrection appearances of Jesus. And Paul's case certainly didn't fit the profile of anything like a conversion disorder.

An *objective vision* is different from a hallucination. For in the former there's something objectively there, unlike hallucinations. According to this theory, what the disciples claimed to have seen after Jesus' crucifixion was not his resurrected body but something else, such as an astral projection. Yet most naturalists would consider an astral projection to be no less inherently miraculous than a resurrection, and that the disciples were convinced it was more than an objective vision also weakens the objective vision theory. Therefore this theory lacks explanatory power because it is unable to account for the disciples' conviction regarding bodily resurrection and because it does not account for the empty tomb. And, frankly, because the theory requires an event no less miraculous than the resurrection, why bother with it?

The legend theory assumes that the "myth" of the resurrection grew over time. This theory lacks explanatory scope because of the empty tomb and lacks plausibility and explanatory power because the claims didn't get bigger as time went on. The resurrection creed in 1 Corinthians 15 was formalized a mere two years, at most, after the event, as we've seen. The evidence that the very earliest Christians claimed the resurrection actually happened is extremely strong.

With such challenges facing typical naturalistic attempts to explain the full set of minimal facts, the next approach is an understandable one: Let's try combining aspects of the theories to enhance their explanatory scope, power and the like. In general, though, such attempts become even more implausible, multiplying the improbabilities involved. Let's take Ehrman's attempt, for example. He says he could provide dozens of alternative scenarios for the various facts in need of explanation, all of them improbable but still more probable than the resurrection. Here's one:

> Jesus gets buried by Joseph of Arimathea. Two of Jesus' family members are upset that an unknown Jewish leader has buried the body. In the dead of night, these two family members raid the tomb, taking the body off to bury it for themselves. But Roman soldiers on the lookout see them carrying the shrouded corpse through the streets, they confront them, and they kill them on the spot. They throw all three bodies into a common burial plot, where within three days these bodies are decomposed beyond recognition. The tomb then is empty. People go to the tomb, they find it empty, they come to think that Jesus was raised from the dead, and they start thinking they've seen him because they know he's been raised because his tomb is empty.[12]

Now, Ehrman admits this is a highly unlikely scenario, but he thinks it has the virtue of explaining the relevant facts without recourse to divine intervention. And he's right, of course, that such a scenario, even if improbable, is possible. In fact, it's a worthwhile exercise to try this yourself, to attempt to generate a purely natural-

---

[12]Ehrman suggests this scenario in the debate with Craig, cited earlier and available online (see n. 4).

istic explanation for all the relevant facts. Invariably the explanation will become highly ad hoc and extremely unlikely, altogether ill equipped to handle all the relevant facts. In Ehrman's scenario, for example, family members who didn't believe in Jesus' divinity during his lifetime would have to find the motive to do this; there would have to have been sufficient time for such a conspiracy to hatch between Friday and Sunday; reports of grave clothes in the tomb would have to be wrong; the Roman guards would have kept mum despite all the subsequent efforts to find out what happened to the body of Jesus; and there's no explanation provided at all of the appearances of Jesus.

Let's suppose this scenario: Joseph of Arimathea took the body of Jesus and first hired helpers to lift it onto a cart to remove to another location. A man is cleaning up the tomb when the women arrive and informs them that Jesus was "lifted up" and taken elsewhere. According to Mark, the women did not know what happened. Startled, afraid, trembling, they say nothing to anyone. But shortly afterward, rumors of the empty tomb are transformed into Jesus being "lifted up," raised from the dead by God. Given the power of belief, the rumors spread and claims of sightings of Jesus multiply. Perhaps a few isolated hallucinations add fuel to the rumors; other appearances involve a confusion of identity; others are exaggerations.

Is this a better explanation than the resurrection? No one scenario really is a good explanation, many would suggest. This scenario is certainly possible, but consider again the confluence of events that would have needed to transpire: there would have had to be major confusion and practically collective amnesia as to where Jesus was buried; Joseph would have had to leave town; Paul would have had to experience an auditory and visual hallucination along with suffering, as Habermas points out, something of a messiah complex; James would have needed to misidentify his own brother; and not a hint of this story would have leaked to confirm suspicions that the resurrection didn't happen. The improbabilities involved multiply to render the scenario extremely implausible. And this seems to be the fate of all the various naturalistic accounts. The one really compelling feature they have is that they don't require the positing of a resurrection, and we'll return to this point in the next section.

For now, though, consider the *resurrection* as a potential explanation. The facts on which virtually all critical scholars are agreed are neatly explained, every one of them. Jesus really died and was buried, causing the disciples to despair and lose hope. Then something sufficiently monumental happened, as it must have, to transform them into bold proclaimers of his resurrection. This message became their central affirmation, proclaimed in the very city in which Jesus had been shortly before killed. Their enemies can't disprove the resurrection, and many people claim to have seen the risen Jesus—even Jesus' own brother, changing him from skeptic to church leader. The church grows, Sunday becomes the new day of worship, and a few years later, Paul too claims to see the post-ascension risen Jesus, eventually going to Jerusalem and meeting with earlier eyewitnesses and confirming that the message he and they were preaching was the same.

It isn't just that the resurrection happens to be the only theory left. Its explanatory scope and power are impeccable because it explains the empty tomb, Jesus' widespread appearances, the conversions of James and Paul, and the disciples' sincere belief in a glorious resurrection rather than a vision of or a resuscitated Jesus. It's plausible because it is consistent with death by crucifixion and early, eyewitness and multiple reports. It doesn't fall prey to ad hoc combinations of unlikelihoods to achieve explanatory scope, power and plausibility. And it's consistent with other evidence of God's existence, which we will discuss closer to the end of this discussion.

On this basis, the claim is that the resurrection is the best explanation for the minimal facts. Both the failure of the naturalistic explanations and the positive reasons to believe in the resurrection render belief in the historicity of the resurrection altogether rational, any elements of ad hoc–ness notwithstanding.

But not so fast. Because critics at this point have a number of points they would like to make. So let's see what they are, for they will enable us to zero in on several important philosophical aspects of this discussion too easily neglected.

SOME SKEPTICAL CHALLENGES

We will treat about seven potential replies by a skeptic at this point. They are not without merit by any stretch of the imagination. It's here, I suggest, rather than at the level of the historical evidence, that atheists have a firmer footing to resist the resurrection argument.

To understand these objections, it's useful to bear in mind the structure of the argument under consideration. It begins with Habermas's minimal facts, historically established. From these we infer, using the criteria of abduction, the best explanation to be the resurrection, which is thought to be better at accounting for the minimal facts than each of the naturalistic explanations on offer. We then infer that the resurrection is the true explanation on the basis of its being the best explanation. So we conclude that the resurrection happened, then we reasonably infer, with a bit of additional argumentation, that Christianity is true.

Note that there are (at least) three inferences involved here: from the minimal facts to the resurrection as the best explanation; from the resurrection being the best explanation to its being the (likely) true explanation; and from the fact of the resurrection to the truth of Christianity. The following objections are liable to deal with any of them, even though we haven't elaborated on the third, in part due to space constraints and in part because it's likely the least controversial.

The seven objections are the a priori dismissal objection, an overriding objection, a probability objection, a margin of victory objection, the Elvis objection, the promissory note objection, and the underdetermination objection. Let's look at each one, starting with the first.

The *a priori dismissal objection* to the resurrection argument denies that the resurrection hypothesis deserves a place among the initial pool of explanation candidates. We can't infer it as the best explanation, therefore, because it's not in the running. By its nature, it is ruled out from the beginning. Ehrman offers a historical variant of this objection by suggesting that it's outside the historian's purview ever to appeal to the miraculous in attempts to figure out what happened historically, because miracles are always less likely than some naturalistic account or other. In this way he embraces a historical variant of the procedure of the methodological naturalism that scientists often endorse in their investigations. To appeal to the supernatural on this view is to give up, to opt for a theistic explanation that leaves further search for naturalistic explanations behind. Ehrman argues that a historian should never do this.[13]

It should be obvious that Habermas would reply that his initial resurrection conclusion doesn't assume it's a miracle, but Ehrman's reply could be recast as saying no conclusion this odd—a man coming back to life—should be allowed among the pool of candidates. The same could be said for each reference to miracles in subsequent objections as well.

Readers acquainted with philosophy should recognize that Ehrman's historical a priori move here is highly reminiscent of David Hume's argument against rational belief in miracles. Since miracles, Hume argued, are by their nature so exceedingly unlikely, naturalistic explanations will always trump them, rendering belief in miracles, especially on the basis of the testimony of others, always irrational.

---

[13]Interesting historical note: Chauncey Wright, an avid antisupernaturalist who exerted a formative influence on thinkers like William James and Charles Peirce, "used the term positive [science], as it is now commonly employed, as a general appellation to designate a whole body of thinkers who in the investigation of nature hold to the methods of induction from the facts of observation, as distinguished from the a priori school who seek in the constitution of the mind the key to the interpretation of the external world," explains his friend Charles Eliot Norton. Fascinating is the role reversal today between the theistic evidentialists and the a priori–driven atheists in this debate. Chauncey Wright, *Philosophical Discussions* (New York: H. Holt, 1877), p. xviii.

You may recall that Habermas accuses Flew of endorsing such an a priori rejection of the miraculous in the debate, and this issue has occurred in each of their debates. But in fact Flew at least denies that his is a categorical rejection of the miraculous. In principle, some kind of evidence would be enough. This means that Flew doesn't exactly fall into this first category, but rather the next, which we're calling an *overriding objection*, and to which we now turn.

This objection doesn't categorically preclude either the metaphysical possibility of miracles or the rational belief in their occurrence, but nonetheless poses a strong enough resistance to rational belief in their occurrence that it can resemble an a priori rejection of their possibility. Barring a miracle beyond all rational doubt, skepticism trumps. It isn't that resurrection doesn't belong in the pool of potential explanation candidates. But because miracles are what they are—events impossible without divine intervention—the evidence for them must be simply overwhelming. Appeals to the miraculous are prima facie implausible in the extreme, so all that is needed to avoid such appeals is a naturalistic explanation that's possible. The naturalistic explanation needn't be plausible, but merely possible.

Recall how Flew and Habermas tend to come to a fork in the road on this issue. Flew suggests possible naturalistic accounts, even if exceedingly unlikely, and thinks that's sufficient. Habermas insists that Flew needs more than remote possibilities, but rather something plausible. This is a crucial divide on this issue, and I think it makes perfect sense if Flew's basic objection is this quasi-Humean, a priori dismissal of the miraculous that is practically categorical if not altogether so. Naturalistic explanations, however remote, are thought to be enough for Flew because miracles are, almost by definition, remoter still.

A third type of response by the skeptic is the *probability objection*. This objection is similar to Alvin Plantinga's critique of Swinburne's argument for theism. In Plantinga's view, Swinburne's arguments for theism and Christianity fall prey to the problem of "diminishing probabilities." Similarly, Swinburne's case for the resurrection involves a series of interlocking reasons. Even if we generously assign a greater than 50-percent probability to each reason, the probability of the ultimate conclusion, the historical reality of the resurrection, is less than 0.5 due to the multiplication of or diminishing probabilities. Recall how in the discussion the moderator once asked if the debate almost boiled down to a comparison of unlikelihoods and improbabilities. Habermas agreed it involved an issue of probabilities versus improbabilities.

But if so, unless the case can be made that the resurrection is more likely than not—that is, that its probability is greater than 0.5—then there may be reason to doubt it *even if* it's the best explanation on offer. So this is a new objection. Here the idea seems to be this: even supposing that we include resurrection in the pool of explanation candidates and even if we concede that resurrection might be the best explanation on offer, we still may have reason to retain skepticism. Unless the resurrection can be shown to be more likely than not, which requires more than showing that it's the best explanation, an atheist can perhaps remain within his or her epistemic rights in suspending judgment on the matter rather than affirming its historicity. In short, we are not justified in inferring that the resurrection is probably true merely because we have shown it is the best explanation of the facts.

Perhaps this example will help. Suppose there's a vat of 500 Ping-Pong balls, 249 of which have the number 1 written on them. The rest are roughly evenly divided; some have 2 written on them, some 3, some 4 and some 5. If I were to reach into the vat and select one Ping-Pong ball randomly and had to place a bet on which number was written on it, it would be very rational to bet on 1. That number is about four times more likely than any other. But it's a different question if I'm asked how confident I can be that I'll select a ball with 1 on it, because in fact it's more likely than not that I won't. Of the balls, 251 have a different number from that. Yes, 1 beats 2, and 1 beats 3, and so on, just as resurrection might beat swoon theory, and resurrection might beat legend. But this doesn't mean that resurrection is more likely true than false any more than selecting a ball with a 1 is more likely than selecting a ball with a different number. And unless more work is done than an abductive case that resurrection wins—unless it can be shown that resurrection is not just the best explanation but more likely true than false—a skeptic can claim, with some legitimacy, to have reason to remain a skeptic. The inference from best explanation to true explanation is open to question.

The *margin of victory* objection might suggest that even if resurrection is the best explanation, its probabilistic margin of victory over its rivals has to be substantial enough to warrant such a huge conclusion—that a dead person came to life again. Ambitious conclusions require extraordinary evidence.[14]

The last several objections countenance the possibility that resurrection might constitute the best explanation because of radical limitations besetting the particular naturalistic explanations so far proposed or some combination of them. But the *Elvis objection* takes a different approach. It denies that resurrection is the best explanation—without bothering to provide a naturalistic alternative. Consider this analogy: Plenty of folks claim to have seen Elvis Presley after his reported death. Suppose we get permission to dig up his grave and discover, as some claim would be the case, the casket is empty. We would therefore have a missing body and alleged appearances, but who among us but a credulous few would consider this to be ample reason to entertain serious doubts about his death? A resurrected or never-dead Elvis would strike us as an epistemically

---

[14]Robert Greg Cavin has further argued that apprehending the full set of implications of a resurrected Jesus—a glorified body with supernatural powers, for example—makes the conclusion in question here even harder to establish on historical grounds alone, which seem ill suited for providing such an inferential basis. But recall that Habermas's resurrection conclusion is less ambitious, so Cavin's criticism wouldn't apply to his case. See Robert Greg Cavin, "Is There Sufficient Historical Evidence to Establish the Resurrection of Jesus?" *Faith and Philosophy* 12, no. 3 (1995): 361-79.

crummy explanation for this information, despite our inability to provide a suitable naturalistic explanation beyond guesswork. The Elvis
scenario thus denies that rejecting resurrection as the best explanation requires a better naturalistic explanation to serve in its stead.

Related to this objection is the *promissory note* objection, which
puts confidence in a naturalistic worldview and the success of science at finding nontheistic explanations of mysterious phenomena,
warranting trust that eventually a naturalistic answer will emerge.
Although no naturalistic explanation suffices for now to account for
Habermas's minimal facts, eventually science will provide the explanation sought for. Habermas might suggest that in the meantime we
should deal with what facts we have and not refrain from following
the evidence where it leads, but skeptics remind him that nonnatu-
ralistic explanations have often been provided for phenomena that
later get accounted for in perfectly naturalistic terms. Isn't that excellent inductive reason to assume that something similar will happen
here? Habermas's confidence in theistic explanations can be matched
by atheists whose principled confidence in naturalistic explanations
is just as high.

One last objection to be mentioned here, without any pretense of
an exhaustive list, is the *underdetermination objection*. Flew flirts
with this objection from time to time, and it basically goes like this:
When it comes to what happened in first-century Palestine, we just
don't know enough to figure it out. Theists aren't stupid for thinking
that a resurrection happened there, and they're not without their reasons for thinking this, but skeptics are entirely right to raise questions about whether the information we have—even granting all of
Habermas's minimal facts—is enough to figure it out. The evidence,
though interesting, leaves room for legitimate doubt. We may never
know what happened there two thousand years ago. Key records that
could have helped may have been irretrievably lost during the Siege
of Jerusalem. We can't know a priori that there's always adequate
historical basis on which to infer just what happened; in fact, we

know this isn't the case. Even if we know a fair bit about the events surrounding the alleged resurrection and appearances, there's no guarantee it is adequate basis to infer what transpired. So where are we? On the basis of the historical facts of which we can be reasonably sure, we advanced Habermas's abductive case for the resurrection, which we then subjected to various skeptical critiques. The argument and these criticisms have broached several important philosophical questions that need to be addressed more carefully if we're going to assess the quality of the resurrection argument, and so that's what I propose we now do.

TEN PHILOSOPHICAL CONCERNS

We are now going to zero in on ten philosophical questions that lurk in the background of this discussion, each making its presence felt at various turns. These are important and controversial aspects of the debate, but too often they go without explicit recognition. So this section should help give them the attention they deserve. The issues to be discussed are methodological naturalism, scientism, the adequacy of naturalism, Hume (on miracles), criteria for miracles and a "god of the gaps" charge, dwindling probabilities, falsifiability, the Elvis analogy, probability versus possibility, and persuadability.

Methodological naturalism. The basic idea behind methodological naturalism is that naturalistic explanations always deserve to be privileged over supernaturalistic ones. This is the sort of philosophical commitment often residing at the base of Flew's resistance to claims smacking of the miraculous. Ehrman's historical variant of it is close to the same idea. What's most important to stress about this methodology is that it is indeed more of a philosophical commitment than a contribution either of science or of history. It's a method by which to uncover naturalistic explanations, and so far as methods go, it's a good place to begin. Where the resurrection is concerned, naturalistic explanations should be explored, and if there's an adequate naturalistic explanation, then it deserves primacy. We all should have a healthy skepticism about alleged miraculous claims. The issue at some point becomes, however, whether supernaturalistic explanations are even in principle allowable. If the answer is no, then the method has potentially been accorded a kind of metaphysical priority that it doesn't rightly deserve, unless of course there's indeed good reason to assume that naturalism is the true worldview.

Scientism. Contrary to the claims of some, science has yet to show that the physical world is all there is. In their 2000 debate on the Inspiration Network, Flew was asked to provide a brief summary of his case for philosophical naturalism. His response was telling: "Well, I don't think it is something that really needs to have a case for it. This is the history of science and the achievement of science. I don't need to produce some argument to show that a great deal has been discovered about the world."[15] Flew is a brilliant philosopher, but clearly at this juncture he wasn't at his best. The inference from "science has taught us about the physical world" to "the physical world is all there is" constitutes a logical leap of indefensible proportions. Yet at this point, unlike more recently, Flew seemed held in the sway of this charming notion of science as having helped establish naturalism.

The idea, though mistaken, is understandable. Science has indeed taught us much about the physical world, and unexplained phenomena attributed to divine agency have often later been explained in naturalistic terms (which, for the record, doesn't preclude divine agency). But we need to be careful not to cross a line here. Science sets out to confine its examination to the physical world, and so it directs its attention to the empirical world. It's tempting, but nonetheless confused, on this basis to infer that the physical world is all that exists, since that's all that science sees. Crossing that line is a philosophical step, not a scientific one, and it effects the transition from science to scientism. Bertrand Russell's famous lines about all

---

[15]Gary R. Habermas and Antony G. N. Flew, *Resurrected? An Atheist and Theist Dialogue*, ed. John F. Ankerberg (Lanham, Md.: Rowman and Littlefield, 2005), p. 61.

the noonday brightness of human genius doomed to extinction being a nearly certain deliverance of science is a paradigmatic example of such scientism. As is Rudolf Bultmann's famous refrain:

> It is impossible to use the electric light and the wireless and to avail ourselves of modern medical and surgical discoveries, and at the same time to believe in the New Testament world of spirits and miracles. We may think we can manage it in our lives, but to expect others to do so is to make the Christian faith unintelligible and unacceptable to the modern world.[16]

Undoubtedly, modern thinkers, often nonphilosophers like the liberal theologian Bultmann here or the New Testament scholar Ehrman, are overly beholden to indecisive arguments against metaphysics or the miraculous advanced by the likes of Kant and Hume when they try to use science or history as justification for philosophical naturalism.

Adequacy of naturalism. The presumed adequacy of naturalism is a huge driving force in the minds of those rigidly skeptical of all miracle claims. It's not necessarily an irrational position to hold; there are very intelligent atheists out there whose secular presuppositions radically differ from my own, but who strike me as fair-minded and intellectually honest. If they hold what they sincerely consider to be very principled reasons for supreme confidence in naturalism to provide all the explanations we need, it's, well, natural for them to put up great resistance against miraculous claims, or even claims likely to point in that direction.

To my thinking, naturalism encounters some severe difficulties. It's challenged in explaining seemingly answered prayers and documented cases of evidentially significant near-death experiences. It fares poorly in accounting for qualia, consciousness, the emergence of life and the start of the universe. It lacks resources in accounting for human reason itself—if we're complicated organic machines

---

[16]Rudolf Bultmann, "The New Testament and Mythology," in *Kerygma and Myth*, ed. Hans Werner Bartsch (New York: Harper and Row, 1961), p. 5.

whose every choice is caused by antecedent conditions and the physical laws of the world. I think naturalism is especially vulnerable when it comes to accounting for such realities as moral regret, moral obligations, moral rights and moral freedom, all of which make considerably more sense from a theistic viewpoint. Naturalism doesn't deserve the sort of unbridled allegiance and undying devotion that some would give it, and it certainly doesn't qualify to be what sets the terms for surrender in this debate.

Suffice it to say that one's prior confidence level in naturalism will greatly shape one's view of the strength of the inference involved in the resurrection argument. Despite my disagreement with atheists, I've acknowledged that their worldview can be a rational one, so I'm willing to concede that the resurrection argument, in and of itself, need not be rationally constraining on them, given their prior convictions that invariably help shape their overall perspective on and appraisal of this argument taken in isolation. However, there can also be an uncritical commitment to naturalism, exhibiting a lack of epistemic humility as well as a dogmatic atheism closed to considering new evidence. Confidence in naturalism should be tempered with the honest recognition that every worldview has its problems, intractable or not, and though naturalism challenges resurrection, so too resurrection challenges naturalism. That rational rejection of the resurrection may be possible doesn't mean that every rejection of it is rational. Nor does it remotely imply that, for certain theists and atheists alike, the case for the resurrection isn't strong and isn't remarkable evidence for the truth of Christianity.

Hume on miracles. David Hume's famous argument against miracles is a notorious reason why many naturalists persist in remaining skeptical even about the most evidentially promising of miracle claims, even though Hume's essay has been severely criticized by many philosophers in recent years. Flew is a perfect example here of someone who's a Hume scholar and who, despite his admission that the resurrection is the strongest miracle claim out there, remains unconvinced. Earlier, looking at the evidence, we considered Hume's undercutting defeaters: considerations that undermine the credibility of those professing to be witnesses of miracles. More relevant to the inferential aspect of the argument, Hume's overriding considerations have already been discussed: it's never or at least very rarely rational to believe in a miracle, because a miracle is so intrinsically unlikely and, in virtue of violating a law of nature, practically impossible. Other explanations, however farfetched or implausible, will always be more likely. Flew himself has admitted that this argument against miracles needs qualifying, and I won't reiterate his caveats here, but I'll briefly mention five objections to Hume (and Flew's amended Hume) that Habermas has raised:

1. Most Humean-styled philosophical objections to miracles are attempts to mount up the data against miracles in an a priori manner (that is, before or in spite of the factual evidence), so that no facts could actually establish their occurrence.

2. These philosophical objections are also mistaken in not allowing for the real possibility of external intervention in nature.

3. These philosophical objections generally treat the laws of nature in an almost Newtonian sense as the final word on what may occur. This overlooks newer views of the laws of nature as statistical generalizations and as consistent with quite odd and unexpected occurrences.

4. Strict empiricism ignores both the empirical (even repeatable) evidence for miracles and the fact that the strict forms of verificational standards are themselves nonverifiable.

5. The philosophical approach of Hume frequently ignores the strong historical evidence for the resurrection of Jesus.[17]

Again, many take Hume's critique of miracles from his influential

---

[17]Gary R. Habermas and Antony G. N. Flew, *Did Jesus Rise from the Dead? The Resurrection Debate*, ed. Terry L. Miethe (San Francisco: Harper & Row, 1987), pp. 16-19.

essay "Of Miracles" as decisive reason to reject miracle claims a priori. Recent critiques of Hume, such as John Earman's *Hume's Abject Failure: The Argument Against Miracles*, have clearly demonstrated that Hume's objections to the miraculous are not only far from decisive, but, indeed, fatally flawed. Hume failed to distinguish, for example, between the intrinsic probability of something like the resurrection, which may well be very low, and the probability of the resurrection in the light of the evidence we have for it, the improbability of having that evidence if the resurrection didn't happen and the low probabilities of naturalistic alternatives, which collectively could render the probability of the resurrection considerably higher than judgments of its intrinsic probability that fail to take such considerations into account. All of this means that merely invoking the name of Hume to discount miracles fails to do anywhere near as much work as some think.

God of the gaps charge. To avoid a "god of the gaps" charge and also recognize the legitimate bias against miracles we should all have, it's incumbent on proponents of the resurrection argument to give principled criteria for legitimate miracle claims. Again, if one is an atheist and has eliminated miracles from the list of explanation candidates a priori or, for practical purposes, nearly a priori, these don't apply. But for those for whom a miracle remains a potential explanation, philosopher Stephen T. Davis has suggested these three criteria: (1) when the available naturalistic explanations all fail and nothing else on the naturalistic horizon seems promising, (2) when the event has moral and religious significance, and (3) when the event in question is consistent with one's background beliefs about the desires and purposes of God, as revealed in the religion to which one is committed (for example, the event occurred after prayer or as an aspect of an epiphany or incarnation).[18]

Again, an atheist must have reasons for thinking that theism is

---

[18]Craig and Lüdemann, *Jesus' Resurrection*, p. 75.

untenable or evidentially suspect in the extreme in order for his or her resistance to the miraculous to be principled; but assuming this is the case, clearly these criteria aren't as helpful in persuading the atheist that the resurrection happened as in convincing the theist that a miracle indeed occurred. This is to some degree unavoidable; the worldview assumptions we bring to our analyses shape our perspectives, and rational people can disagree. Even if the resurrection argument might provide to atheists some evidence for theism and Christianity, perhaps even enough to make their decision to convert epistemically permissible, I suspect that by itself it rarely rationally constrains them to believe.

Dwindling probabilities. Earlier I mentioned that Alvin Plantinga offers a critique of a version of Swinburne's historical and evidentialist argument for theism, a critique that can also be thought to apply to a case for the resurrection. Several points need addressing here. In *Philosophia Christi*, Timothy McGrew and later he and Lydia McGrew wrote some critical analyses of Plantinga's arguments that seems effectively to rebut them.[19] The discussion culminated in Plantinga seeming to back off some of his earlier antievidentialism and acknowledge that some historical arguments for tenets of the Christian faith are quite impressive, Habermas's among them. McGrew effectively demonstrated that Swinburne's historical argument for Christian theism, appropriately nuanced, can evade the dwindling probabilities objection. Evidence for the resurrection itself counts as part of the total evidence for theism. As the McGrews put it,

---

[19]Timothy McGrew, "Has Plantinga Refuted the Historical Argument?" *Philosophia Christi* 6, no. 1 (2004): 7-25; Alvin Plantinga, "Historical Arguments and Dwindling Probabilities: A Response to Timothy McGrew," *Philosophia Christi* 8, no. 1 (2006): 7-22; Timothy and Lydia McGrew, "On the Historical Argument: A Rejoinder to Plantinga," *Philosophia Christi* 8, no. 1 (2006): 23-38. Incidentally, that same 2006 issue of *Philosophia Christi* contains Stephen T. Davis's excellent review article of *The Empty Tomb: Jesus Beyond the Grave*, a collection of essays by resurrection skeptics (pp. 38-63). Despite its huge faults, this book, as Davis notes, does mark the attempt by skeptics to answer the evidentialists who have been advancing some sophisticated and powerful arguments for the historicity of the resurrection.

If the historical evidence for the resurrection is relevant to theism by way of its relevance to the resurrection, we must take it into account in order to find the probability of theism on all evidence in the first place. And in that case, we have already taken both that evidence and its impact on the resurrection into account and cannot be trying to find out how much of it we need for evaluating the probability of the resurrection.[20]

They also point out how it's strange that Plantinga critiques Swinburne by resorting to successive multiplications in the Theorem of Total Probability when Swinburne is the foremost living exponent of the use of Bayes's theorem in the philosophy of religion.[21] The only clear-eyed approach to the question of assessing theism and the case for the resurrection, two mutually relevant propositions, is to examine in as much detail as possible the evidence pertinent, directly or indirectly, to each of them, the McGrews insist. There's no substitute, in other words, for examining the evidence itself, rather than deciding beforehand what we think of the evidence based on questionable probability assignments.

Of course, a tricky aspect about examining the evidence is that the reasons for overly rosy or unduly pessimistic probability assignments may be skewing one's objective assessment of the quality of the evidence in question. Using Bayes's theorem, for example, an atheist is likely to end up thinking the resurrection less likely than not, and many theists, lacking the same a priori confidence in naturalism and an automatic rejection of anything smacking of the miraculous, would

---

[20]McGrew and McGrew, "On the Historical Argument," p. 29.

[21]The McGrews stress that Swinburne has repeatedly rejected Plantinga's characterization of his (Swinburne's) argument as involving the evaluation of the probabilities of both theism and the resurrection against an univocal set comprising all of our background evidence but in which, nevertheless, we must first evaluate the probability of theism on total evidence. See Richard Swinburne, "Natural Theology, Its 'Dwindling Probabilities' and 'Lack of Rapport,'" *Faith and Philosophy* 4 (2004): 541-42. See also Swinburne, *The Resurrection of God Incarnate* (New York: Oxford University Press, 2003), pp. 30-31.

be hard-pressed to think the resurrection less likely than not.[22] And similar honest biases will be reflected in their assessment of the quality of the evidential case Habermas would construct.

What we think about the power of naturalistic explanations (perhaps yet to be discovered) and how likely the resurrection is on the basis of background beliefs deeply depend on prior philosophical commitments. In one sense this is entirely obvious, but if the disparity in worldviews reveals something epistemically legitimate, and not just something psychological, it may indicate that, even if the resurrection provides excellent evidence to many theists and some atheists that Christianity is true, it may not be irrational for some to resist it, at least when considering it in isolation. Again, though, this possibility doesn't indicate that every resistance or reason for doubt or skepticism is equally rational, or even rational at all. It would be deeply surprising if this were the case. Habermas, for example, distinguishes between doubts evidential, emotional and volitional; once the evidential questions are settled, the emotional and volitional sources of doubt become all the more important to consider.[23]

Incidentally, recall the earlier example of how 1 beats 2 and beats 3 and beats 4, but without being more likely than not. One conclusion to draw from that illustration is that, even if the resurrection provides the better explanation than any naturalistic hypothesis on offer, we can rationally refrain from believing it for its intrinsic unlikelihood. But another possibility to consider is the exact opposite conclusion: that it's rational to choose 1 shows, by parity of reasoning, it may be rational to believe in the resurrection even if it cannot be shown to be more likely than not, much less that its probability considerably beats both 50 percent and the competition, so long as it better explains the

---

[22]In a short appendix, I will demonstrate an application of Bayes's theorem. I reserve it until then to give the symbol and number-phobic among you the chance to avoid it, and the proud, pocket-protector-wearing geeks among you the chance to indulge your number-crunching tastes to your heart's content.

[23]See Gary R. Habermas, *Dealing with Doubt* (Chicago: Moody Press, 1990), and *The Thomas Factor* (Nashville: Broadman & Holman, 1998).

relevant phenomena than its rivals. The fact that the explanatory values of logically incompatible alternative naturalistic hypotheses can't be combined into a single explanatory value of its own surpassing that of resurrection bolsters this case. And if so, this would show that probability calculations may well be far less important than the force of Habermas's abductive inference. And again, this would drive us to consider the actual historical case to be made and not just to dismiss it ahead of time by a priori and perhaps altogether uninformed, presumptuous or inscrutable probability assignments.[24]

Falsifiability. Flew is the very philosopher who conceived the principle of falsifiabililty. He saw his initial 1950 essay on this, "Theology and Falsification," earlier read at a Socratic Club meeting run by C. S. Lewis at Oxford University, as an effort to argue both for atheism and against logical positivism. He didn't intend the piece to pose a test that a claim must pass to be meaningful, but merely a test that a claim must pass to be reasonable. If nothing even in principle can show a claim to be false, it doesn't pass the test of falsifiability and is worthy of rejection on this basis. It may still be coherent, but it's not rational to believe.

Not surprisingly, then, given what borders Flew's a priori resistance to the miraculous, Habermas challenges him on the question of falsifiability. Is Flew's conviction that the resurrection didn't happen a falsifiable belief? More generally, is his aversion to miracles falsifi-

---

[24]Tim McGrew adds another smart twist to the connection between probabilistic arguments and abductive inferences. Two theories might account equally well for each fact to be explained, but one of the theories might possess a greater epistemic set of virtues by providing a more unified picture. A theory that accounts for each individual fact, such as an elaborate secular scenario providing independent naturalistic explanations for Paul's experience, the alleged appearances, the empty tomb and the like, nonetheless suffers the defect of mounting improbabilities. The explanations provided aren't connected to one another, nor do they increase the likelihood of the others. A Bayesian analysis can thereby bolster an abductive case for the resurrection by illustrating its comparative unifying power by showing how it simply packages the conjunction of data more effectively and by the way its explanations mutually increase the probabilities of the others. See his "Confirmation, Heuristics, and Explanatory Reasoning" at <homepages.wmich.edu/~mcgrew/bjps.htm>.

able? Could anything in principle change his mind? This is where Flew ostensibly distinguishes his opposition to the miraculous from a purely a priori rejection of the miraculous by some. No, he claims that, at least in theory, something sufficiently dramatic could convince him that a miracle took place. If God, for example, were to speak all the world over in a loud, booming voice, that might do it, he's suggested. Habermas presses him on this issue, and at moments Flew's words sound awfully like an a priori resistance come what may, his protestations that his views are falsifiable notwithstanding.

Interestingly, three points from the writings of the French philosopher Blaise Pascal ought to be mentioned here, because the discussion until now has raised three related epistemic challenges to the resurrection inference, to which Pascal offers resources for responding. Recall the atheist who might wish to suggest that, unless the resurrection can be shown to be more likely than not, the most reasonable response would be to suspend judgment. Pascal might suggest that what such a person needs to remember is that suspending judgment on this vital matter is not maintaining neutrality, nor is it the equivalent of staying at home rather than frequenting the betting track, but rather a decision with big implications. It is his bet. Relatedly, the sheer size of the claim of the resurrection argument requires commensurately big evidence. True enough. But Pascal would also remind us that the size of the claim is also the reason why so much is at stake here. It's not a truth we want to miss out on because of an excessively narrow evidentialism so concerned to avoid error that it precludes our coming to know truths that may well be there to be known, truths that couldn't be more existentially central to the enduring questions about the human condition and the nature of reality.

William James once said the strict secularists and naturalists, the zealous knights of Ockham's razor, feared superstition, while he himself feared desiccation, an emaciated worldview stripped bare of its most interesting and important features and reduced to a drab physicalist picture alone. Pascal shared such a concern. And as to why the evidence isn't yet more compelling than it is, nor the inference yet not stronger, Pascal would remind us that God may have reasons for retaining a measure of hiddenness, so that he doesn't merely inundate us with his light of revelation, thus coercing our will. Rather he offers just enough light for us to respond to it with intellectual integrity, both with our minds and with our hearts and wills. After all, doesn't it make sense that God's about more than just testing how good we are at assessing evidence? His separation of the wheat from the chaff likely has relatively little to do with that.

Elvis analogy. Recall the Elvis analogy that calls into question the duty of naturalists to provide a workable naturalistic alternative to the resurrection. The body is missing, suppose, and various reasonable people claim to have seen Elvis alive. Either Elvis has risen from the dead or never died in the first place. We can't explain the missing body and the alleged appearances, yet we consider ourselves justified to refrain from positing a theistic explanation or any supernatural one. Doesn't this show that Habermas's demand that Flew provide a naturalistic explanation of the resurrection is misguided?

No, for there are numerous relevant and powerful disanalogies between the Jesus case and the Elvis case. The sightings of Elvis aren't widespread. If, moreover, the body of Elvis was never buried in the first place, as some suggest, there's not as much evidence of his death as in the case of Jesus. Elvis didn't predict his own death, and his death didn't take place in the rich theological context that Jesus' death did, making sense of the event and imbuing it with a sort of moral and spiritual significance entirely lacking in the case of Elvis. Nor do Elvis-is-alive claimants seriously risk martyrdom for their attestations.

What the Elvis case shows, quite simply, is that the principle needs tweaking that says we must always know the naturalistic explanation of an event before we're justified to reject a miracle claim. That principle admits of exceptions, as in the Elvis case. But the disanalogies between the Elvis and Jesus cases are huge, rendering considerably more pressing the responsibility to come up with a better naturalistic account than what's been provided so far. That some actually think the Elvis case serves to suggest anything else relevant to this discussion frankly serves as powerful evidence that they are inclined to trivialize the resurrection argument in a way that simply isn't justified. When the evidence is clearly best explained by a resurrection *and* the naturalistic hypotheses on offer are patently weak, as in the Jesus case but not the Elvis case, inferences to resurrection are justified.

Probability versus possibility. Flew and Habermas consistently uphold a different evidential standard. When it comes to the rival naturalistic hypotheses, Flew time and again wishes to maintain that mere possibilities, however remote, are enough. Habermas presses him on the issue by insisting that this isn't so, that genuinely plausible naturalistic accounts are required. This is a crucial fork in the road that recurs time and again. I don't pretend to adjudicate it, but simply to point it out and to suggest that the reason for it is simple. They're approaching this from two rather different worldviews. As a committed atheist (as of this debate) who treads the verge of an a priori rejection of all miraculous claims, Flew thinks the possibilities are enough, because no matter how improbable they are, they're more probable than Jesus coming back to life. Habermas is a principled theist with legitimate reservations about Humean-styled objections to miracles and numerous reasons to reject the adequacy of naturalism with its promissory notes of eventual explanations for every last phenomenon. He thinks, and properly so, that more than bare naturalistic possibilities are necessary to answer his abductive argument and subsequent case for Christianity. It may not be impossible, but the rigorous effort to show which of these competing sets of presuppositions is the more philosophically defensible is a huge challenge. I have my own convictions on the matter; readers are encouraged to draw their own conclusions. I'd contend, though, that this is one of the deeper underlying debates at play here, and disputes about the resurrection argument are just specific instances of this more general disagreement.

Persuadability. This brings us to an important point about debates of this nature, debates that are really quite important and valuable. They nonetheless have their limits. They are effective at unearthing some of the deeper disagreements involved, which aren't likely to be resolved easily or quickly. This is why folks rarely change their mind after hearing just one debate. If you bring prior assumptions to a debate, those assumptions shape how you hear and assess the arguments. This is as true on the one side of the debate as on the other. Over time our minds may change, but rarely on the spot.

Again, in the face of the challenges that the resurrection argument has to overcome, I'd personally be rather surprised if it in isolation would be enough to persuade a committed, intelligent, principled atheist to change his or her mind. Moreover, I think potentially an atheist would be within his or her epistemic rights to retain some obstinacy on the matter. The resurrection argument, in my estimation, is a powerful one, but works best as part of a broader cumulative case for theism generally and Christianity particularly. Consequently, it is much more likely, and understandably so, to persuade one who's already a theist than the stalwart, smart atheist, even if the argument provides substantial evidence to the atheist that indeed God exists and a miracle took place in first-century Palestine.

And now that our sketch of the relevant underlying philosophical issues involved in this debate is done, we're ready to return the discussion back to Antony Flew, as averse as he may be to our doing so, for much of what we've said here bears relevance to his ongoing journey. He remains an enigmatic and fascinating figure whose story is altogether compelling. Since there have been significant developments in his intellectual pilgrimage since this last debate, evidence of which sprang up in its immediate aftermath, it's time to assess both where he is now and where he may be headed.

WHERE FLEW IS

Not long after their third debate, Flew told Habermas he was considering theism, and a year to the month after the Cal Poly debate, Flew told Habermas that indeed he had become a theist. He now believed in God. Did that mean that Flew had become a Christian? No. Like C. S. Lewis, he had merely become a theist (a Deist, in Flew's case). In Lewis's case, of course, he would eventually become a Christian. Whether or not Flew does remains to be seen.

What changed his mind? What convinced Flew that God indeed exists? Habermas interviewed him about it, and that exchange was eventually published in *Philosophia Christi* and reprinted here in this book. Not long after that, Flew, with Roy Abraham Varghese, wrote *There Is a God: How the World's Most Notorious Atheist Changed His Mind.*[25] Habermas's review essay of that book has been reprinted here as well, but let's quickly review some of the main reasons behind this dramatic shift in Flew's thinking. Then, in the final portion of this chapter, we'll connect the discussion back up with the argument for the resurrection and consider how this could or perhaps should change matters.

Flew is a brilliant philosopher, but it bears repeating that his conversion to theism is no sure evidence that theism is true. Flew himself writes that "a person can be persuaded by an abominable argument and remain unconvinced by one that ought to be accepted."[26] Great philosophers can make mistakes, and even if Flew himself has followed the evidence where he honestly thinks it leads, that doesn't show that theism is true. All we can do, epistemically, is our best, and though Flew's story is dramatic, there have been theists who've renounced their faith, too, for what they thought were intellectually principled reasons. This isn't a matter of trying desperately to enlist a big name to the theistic cause, despite the fact that Flew writes that

---

[25]Antony Flew and Roy Abraham Varghese, *There Is a God: How the World's Most Notorious Atheist Changed His Mind* (New York: HarperCollins, 2007).
[26]Ibid., p. 41.

his now-deceased Oxford-trained, Wesleyan Methodist minister father would be "hugely delighted by my present view on the existence of a God—not least because he would consider this a great help to the cause of the Christian church."[27]

Nonetheless, it's interesting to note why Flew thought that indeed the evidence leads to theism, especially at a time when a breed of "new atheists" has emerged—from Christopher Hitchens to Richard Dawkins to Sam Harris—who repeatedly insist that to embrace religion is the very paradigm of irrationality. In this connection, it's interesting to see that Flew allowed Varghese to write an appendix to their book in which Varghese took on such atheists, who now stand in rather stark contrast to Flew. Rather than demonizing religious adherents or casting them as intellectually challenged, Flew has spent time debating and dialoguing with the best and brightest of Christian philosophers, from Habermas to Alvin Plantinga to Richard Swinburne to William Lane Craig to Brian Leftow. Rhetorically flashy indictments of the stupidity of theists hold little sway for Flew, as he's intentionally spent time with some of its brightest representatives rather than remaining content to issue broad-brush stereotypes based on its dimmest.

What has transpired in Flew's intellectual journey of late is that he has felt the force of general revelation. He insists that he remains unpersuaded by special revelation; the resurrection, and so Christianity, therefore, is still unconvincing to him. But the case for God from general revelation, he thinks, is strong. He's not convinced that there's any life after death, so he wishes to put to rest conjectures that his age has provided the incentive for this transformation. He affirms that the book written with the help of Varghese expresses his own views, despite his advanced years, so criticisms in some quarters of his mental decline seem rather unfair, though, in truth, Flew himself once intimated as much about A. J. Ayer after his famous "near-death

---

[27]Ibid., p. 16.

experience" and Ayer's theistic interpretation of it—an experience that still didn't convince Ayer to reject his atheism.

Flew cites Kant's famous identification of the three great questions of philosophy: God, freedom and immortality. Flew has definitely moved on two of the three. Earlier in his career he embraced a compatibilist view of free will, the sort of freedom consistent with our being determined to act in just the way we do at each moment of our lives—and a view of freedom that precludes our ability to do otherwise. Long prior to his conversion to theism, Flew had changed his mind on the tenability of compatibilism, now sounding much like Roderick Chisholm on the matter, a good indicator that he retains a flexibility in his philosophical convictions. Flew says that this incompatibilist "conversion" is at least as significant as his theistic turn. So far he has yet to budge on the immortality issue, the third of Kant's big three philosophical questions.

In 1966 Flew published *God and Philosophy*, in which he argued against the design, cosmological and moral arguments for God's existence. The strongest argument against God's existence was the problem of evil, in his estimation. He also raised questions about identification and individuation in theism, and he seems to take some pride that his questions helped produce such intelligent work by philosophers like Swinburne and Copleston in their attempts to provide answers, not to mention heady responses by Plantinga in answering other concerns of his. He now considers this 1966 work to be something of a "historical relic," important in its time but early in the discussion. Now, despite his ongoing presumption of atheism, he insists that "given grounds for belief in a God, theists commit no philosophical sin in so believing! The presumption of atheism is, at best, a methodological starting point, not an ontological conclusion."[28]

Among Flew's convictions that bolstered his atheism through the years was his belief that the Bible taught strict predestination, that an

---

[28]Ibid., p. 56.

omnipotent God could have made everyone freely choose the good and that the universe could be eternal, to name a few. One by one these convictions were undermined, as Flew chronicles in *There Is a God*. And then, in 2004, in a conference in New York, around the time of hearing physicist Gerry Schroeder's convincing argument against the "monkey theorem"—the possibility of life arising by chance using the analogy of a multitude of monkeys banging away on computer keyboards and eventually ending up writing a Shakespearean sonnet—Flew announced his acceptance of a God, to the surprise of many.

Flew had come to see the danger of dogmatic atheism to be the way it closes itself off from certain questions, like the search for an explanation of why the world exists. A mere no-nonsense acceptance of brute facts is no explanation and should carry no special authority. Developments in science, in part, led Flew toward acceptance of a divine explanation for various phenomena, and he now finds himself asking his former fellow-atheists the question that used to be posed to him: "What would have to occur or to have occurred to constitute for you a reason to at least consider the existence of a superior Mind?"[29]

The picture of the world that has emerged from modern science has spotlighted three dimensions of nature that Flew thinks point to God. We will mention them here without reiterating his elaborations. The fact that nature obeys laws, the fact that intelligently organized and purpose-driven beings arose from nature, and the very existence of nature itself, along with a renewed study of the classical philosophical arguments, convinced Flew. He emphasizes that when he asks philosophical questions of this scientific picture and draws philosophical conclusions, he's thinking like a philosopher. He need not be a scientist to learn something philosophically interesting from it, and indeed being a scientist does not necessarily enable someone

---

[29]Ibid., p. 88.

to think philosophically about science. He quotes Einstein here, in fact: "The man of science is a poor philosopher."[30]

The God to which the evidence pointed was the God of Aristotle. Flew admits to being most influenced by David Conway's argument for God's existence, and Conway argues, interestingly, that the God of Aristotle bears a striking resemblance to the God of the Judeo-Christian tradition. Flew notes this, without disagreeing, though he goes on to stress that his own journey has not led him to the God of any particular religion. Again, his pilgrimage is the result of natural theology alone, and whereas he's changed his mind on certain versions of the cosmological and teleological arguments, in light of the scientific evidence, the moral argument has yet to impress him. This is why Flew at this point is most inclined to dub himself a Deist.

Again, what convinced Flew from the realm of science was not science itself, but philosophy. He came to see the most relevant issues involved as philosophical ones, not merely scientific. From big bang cosmology to indications of a fine-tuned universe to the physical constants, he began to see the explanatory efficacy of a divine, creative intelligence. Coupled with the ground-breaking work on theism among analytic philosophers like Thomas Tracy and Brian Leftow, Flew's intellectual pilgrimage to theism seemed justified.

He still feels the force of the problem of evil, but it doesn't stand in the way of his theism because of his deistic conception of God. Although he thinks of God as self-existent, immutable, immaterial, omnipotent and omniscient, he also thinks of God as essentially impersonal and not particularly morally significant. An Aristotelian God wouldn't intervene in the world to do away with evil, so the presence of evil doesn't serve as evidence against such a God. A good God probably would intervene more, unless perhaps if the free-will defense goes through, but he suggests that such a defense depends on "the prior acceptance of a framework of divine revelation, the idea

---

[30]Albert Einstein, *Out of My Later Years* (New York: Philosophical Library, 1950), p. 58.

that God has revealed himself." On whether God has revealed himself in history, Flew remains open to the possibility, but so far he is unconvinced. And as far as the resurrection goes, it's perhaps significant that he asked New Testament scholar N. T. Wright to write an appendix on the very subject. Flew writes in the final chapter, "As I have said more than once, no other religion enjoys anything like the combination of a charismatic figure like Jesus and a first-class intellectual like St. Paul. If you're wanting omnipotence to set up a religion, it seems to me that this is the one to beat!"[31]

He ends his book with these words: "Some claim to have made contact with this Mind. I have not—yet. But who knows what could happen next? Someday I might hear a Voice that says, 'Can you hear me now?'"[32]

So let's conclude our treatment by discussing the case for the resurrection in light of Flew's conversion.

WHY FLEW SHOULD BECOME A CHRISTIAN

My section title is meant to be a bit provocative, but only in a semiserious way. Who knows what will happen next in Flew's pilgrimage? He might trip at King's Cross Station and end up at Hogwarts for all I know. But his is certainly an interesting story, and we're naturally curious how it will play out. So allow me to tie several threads of our discussion together and, most importantly, bring to bear the relevance of Flew's conversion to theism on our discussion of the resurrection. Although I will offer some reasons that Flew's conversion to Christianity wouldn't be surprising, I fancy myself neither a detective nor a prognosticator, and wherever he comes down on these issues, we all need to respect his intellectual freedom.

The resurrection is clearly on Flew's mind. As mentioned earlier, in his latest book he invited Wright to lay out some key findings of his (Wright's) latest eight-hundred-page tome on the resurrection.

---

[31]Flew, *There Is a God*, p. 157.
[32]Ibid.

Flew says that Wright's argument and Varghese's appendix on the new atheists are both examples of reasoning that led him to change his mind about God's existence. He also says, interestingly, that they give readers some "insight into the direction of my continuing journey." He also hopes that they, along with his reflections on why theism is philosophically preferable, constitute "an organic whole that provides a powerful new vision of the philosophy of religion."[33] Perhaps Flew's impact on the world of religious philosophy has only just begun.

Flew retains skepticism toward the resurrection, despite the fact that he believes "the resurrection is more impressive than any by the religious competition." Much of his critique tends to dwell on historical matters: lack of contemporary evidence, reliability of group appearances, little physical detail of the resurrection and so on. Despite this, he admits to being more open now to at least certain claims of divine revelation or intervention. "In point of fact," he writes, "I think that the Christian religion is the one religion that most clearly deserves to be honored and respected whether or not its claim to be a divine revelation is true."[34] Besides historical concerns, Flew also still thinks "the occurrence of miracles cannot be known from historical evidence, and this discredits the claim that the resurrection can be known as a fact of history."[35] So despite a degree of openness to Christianity, he isn't quite convinced.

Wright's case, which has several interesting features, won't be repeated here, largely because it's more heavily geared toward answering various historical concerns and questions. And based on what we've seen so far in our study, it seems to me that that debate has largely been won by the likes of Wright and Habermas. If I were to suggest a strategy to my atheist friends who want to resist the resurrection, I would counsel them to focus their case somewhere other

---

[33]Ibid., p. 160.
[34]Ibid., p. 185.
[35]Ibid., p. 186.

than the historical evidence. Those who tangle with Habermas and company on such issues must swim hard upstream. The historical evidence on which the resurrection inference is based is substantial. The remaining debate is inferential, whether or not the inference to the resurrection is a good one. Just as Flew sees aspects of modern science and infers that something substantively philosophical can be said, Habermas's historical case is a fascinating one, and we can learn from it, but how much we can learn raises philosophical questions that have to be answered so the force of the historical case can be fully felt.

Let's return to the issue of Habermas's metaphysically thin resurrection conclusion—by which I don't mean the evidence is thin, but the claim unambitious, stripped of as much of its miraculous content as possible—the claim merely that Jesus, having been dead, was later alive. Even if atheists accept the historical facts on which Habermas bases his case, many of them will likely resist his conclusion. The inference won't convince. Now, in one sense this point is obvious and trivial. Atheists aren't theists; they see things differently and, unless they are willing to stop being atheists, they won't accept theistic conclusions. But is their resistance necessarily irrational? Is the only reason for their resistance psychological? I tend to think they are not necessarily being irrational and that there may be more to their resistance than simply something psychological. For the claim that Jesus was alive, after having been dead, is no garden-variety historical claim. It likely involves a miracle and thus entails the falsity of naturalism. That's a lot to swallow for a principled atheist!

Incidentally, Habermas's modus operandi here might be thought to allay Flew's concern that we can't know from historical evidence that a miracle occurred. For Habermas doesn't wish to argue initially for a miracle, but simply that Jesus was alive, whether or not that was a miracle. It's a smart strategy, but Jesus being alive after being dead most likely involves a miracle claim, and assessment of miracle claims involves more than the resources of history. It involves philosophical judgments about possibility and impossibility, plausibility and implausibility, probabilities and improbabilities, considerations about what constitutes best explanations, and the like. Evidence for Jesus being alive after having been dead needs to be better than evidence for garden-variety historical events that don't pose so deep a challenge to a naturalistic worldview. Without it, naturalists, or even certain theists, seem potentially within their epistemic rights to refrain from inferring the resurrection as the best explanation of Habermas's historical facts.

Interestingly, we *do* seem to have considerably better evidence for the resurrection than for many historical claims we take for granted as fact—Caesar crossing the Rubicon, for example. So we both need and have better evidence for the resurrection, but the question remains, do we have as much and as good evidence as we need? And that seems to invite a philosophical question, not merely an historical one. So there's a sense in which I agree with Flew here (and Habermas, for slightly different reasons, would too): history alone perhaps can't establish miracle claims. This is why Habermas gives additional evidence on which to base the inference from resurrection to miracle. Flew seems to think more evidence is needed than we have, but what I rather suspect is that his resistance is at root more philosophical than historical. When he was an atheist and committed naturalist, this made more sense. His background assumptions would strongly disincline him to believe anything supernatural was going on, his failure to provide better naturalistic alternatives notwithstanding. His naturalism understandably fueled background assumptions about the likelihood of naturalistic explanation and the unlikelihood of a miracle event, rendering his practical a priori resistance to the resurrection sacrosanct.

It was in response to the entrenched naturalism of certain of Habermas's interlocutors that a few years ago he began to build an evidential case of near-death experiences to erode such confidence in naturalism. This very effort by Habermas shows that he sees that the case for the resurrection is made stronger when it's combined with other considerations, like arguments against naturalism. He admits the resurrection argument ideally goes hand in hand with classical arguments for God's existence from natural theology as well. For theists are much less likely to construct an a priori or practical a priori wall of resistance to the miraculous.

But there's the rub with Flew. He's no atheist anymore. His a priori resistance to the resurrection should radically weaken. In fact, he would admit as much to Habermas in their various debates: that if he were a theist the case for the resurrection would become much stronger for him. But he became a theist while still resisting the resurrection and a conversion to Christianity. For someone who has thought this much about the resurrection argument, who has admitted its force and strength, and who is now a theist, this borders on the surprising. His conversion to Christianity would be much less surprising, I contend.

Again, a committed naturalist who performs a Bayes's theorem calculation on the likelihood of the resurrection could plausibly come out thinking that the resurrection is less likely than not. If naturalists end up calculating that the resurrection event is substantially less likely than not, that gives them solid prima facie reason to resist an abductive case for the resurrection. It's even messier than this, in fact, for their negative appraisal of the abductive case will largely emanate from the same source as their initial probability assignments. Some might wish to suggest that such individuals are being irrational, are too beholden to Humean a priori resistance to the miraculous, dishonest in assessing the quality of the historical case.[36]

I am not going to make that argument. For present purposes I'm happy to assume such folks are being as honest as they can be, and they just happen to see things differently. But now take a theist instead. The theist, unless the theism in question demands it, can't in

---

[36]Habermas and Stephen T. Davis have locked horns on the issue of how rationally constraining a case for the resurrection is. See, for example, Habermas's "Knowing that Jesus' Resurrection Occurred: A Response to Davis," *Faith and Philosophy* 2, no. 3 (1985): pp. 295-302.; and Davis's response in his *Risen Indeed: Making Sense of the Resurrection* (Grand Rapids: Eerdmans, 1993), pp. 170-74.

intellectual honesty assign a low probability to the likelihood of the resurrection on the basis of his or her background assumptions. Unless a low probability is assigned to theism in general, an assignment of low probability to the resurrection is altogether presumptuous, even if there aren't any particular grounds for assigning it a high antecedent probability. Similarly, in light of the spectacular failures of naturalistic hypotheses in accounting for the full set of Habermas's minimal facts, a theist can't in good conscience assign a very high probability to the best naturalistic hypothesis to account for such facts. A theist, in other words, applying Bayes's theorem, will be very hard-pressed to think the resurrection is less likely than not. That result, conjoined with a decisive abductive case for the resurrection, makes it considerably harder for the theist rationally to resist the resurrection hypothesis than for the atheist. Even more so for theists like Flew who admit the power of natural theology. The atheist may not be irrational to resist the resurrection if the case for it is considered in isolation, but such a theist may well be. A Deist perhaps not; but resurrection challenges Deism no less than Deism challenges resurrection.

Flew repeatedly emphasized in debates with Habermas that the resurrection case is stronger for the theist, and now he's a theist. He admitted that the resurrection argument would be stronger when combined with aspects of natural theology, and now he's been convinced by natural theology that God exists, but still he resists. Why?

I don't presume to know, but I would like to offer a few possibilities. Recall that Flew has found convincing certain cosmological and teleological arguments for God's existence, after previously resisting them and finding them wanting. But he retains his skepticism when it comes to the moral argument. In various places he offers a few reasons for this. An Aristotelian God is more easily reconcilable with the suffering in the world, for a deistic God wouldn't feel any moral need to intervene. A free-will defense, which he seems drawn to, nonetheless is troubling for him because he thinks it depends on specific revelation in which he can't believe. He resists C. S. Lewis's moral argument on the basis that aspects of the world are hard to make sense of if God is perfectly good. And he often seems to equate a classical monotheistic and Christian conception of God with a pre-destinationist God who inexplicably relegates some to an eternal hell for lives they couldn't have avoided. In fact, he accuses Lewis, as John Beversluis does, of opting for an Ockhamistic voluntarism[37] later in life, after having championed a moral argument for God's existence earlier. Besides which, if morality were to depend on God, God would be its justification, Flew says, which would lead to, at most, pruden-tial reasons to be moral, based on the prospects of punishment for failure to comply.

Thus construed, his resistance to the moral argument makes good sense. Until he thinks of God as personal and moral, rather than merely intellectual and impersonal, his resistance to special revela-tion will probably remain intact. He will continue to be convinced by teleological and cosmological arguments, but not the moral one; and he will continue to have changed his mind about God and compati-bilism, but not the afterlife. His resistance to the resurrection will continue holding sway.

For such reasons, I contend his real resistance to the resurrection is philosophical, and the best answer is philosophical. Conducting the discussion at this level may get him over this preliminary hump and enable him to feel the historical force of Habermas's inference. This may be an example where natural theology can come to the assistance of the resurrection argument, and their resultant cumulative force can exceed that of either argument taken in isolation. So what might be said to address this cluster of moral concerns Flew entertains?

Recall that Flew suggested that a free-will defense to the problem of evil presupposes special revelation. In Habermas's review essay of Flew's book, he understandably raises a question about this, making

---

[37]Such voluntarism affirms the horn of the Euthyphro dilemma that says that whatever God says is moral is moral in virtue of his saying it, which raises various arbitrariness and vacuity objections.

the point that a Deist could believe in free will, but I'm going to make a different point. If we as human beings are genuinely free, able to do otherwise and the like, this is very difficult to reconcile with a naturalistic picture, for reasons obvious enough there's no need to repeat them here. Such freedom would enable us to be morally significant agents. Now Flew seems to think the evidence for our possessing such agency is strong, so let's suppose he embraces such a notion that we have such freedom, and especially such moral freedom. He's also a strong believer that some things are morally right and some morally wrong, that moral duties exist in a strongly prescriptively binding sense. A rough-and-ready version of the moral argument asks us to consider such possibilities, then: moral obligations, moral rights, moral freedom, moral regret. How can we make genuine sense of any of these realities in a world in which all that we are, ultimately, is a collocation of atoms fortuitously arranged? Flew has felt the evidential force of the laws of nature, the existence of something rather than nothing, human consciousness, the efficacy of reason and the emergence of life as evidence for a divine Mind. Why not the existence of the moral law as well?

The reason there may be resistance is that yielding to the force of this argument points to a God who's good and loving, no mere impersonal clockmaker. And it brings front and center again the problem of evil. Now regarding this admittedly difficult issue a few words are in order. In principle this could indeed be a deal breaker for theism. If the sufferings in the world were enough or bad enough, we would likely be rational to infer that a good God doesn't exist. Incidentally Lewis never denied this inference. This is why I think Flew commits the same mistake Beversluis does in characterizing the later Lewis as an Ockhamist. I've made that case elsewhere and won't repeat it here.[38] Suffice it to say, suggesting that we don't live in a world

---

[38]David Baggett, "Is Divine Iconoclast as Bad as Cosmic Sadist?" in *C.S. Lewis as Philosopher: Truth, Goodness and Beauty*, ed. David Baggett, Gary R. Habermas and Jerry L. Walls (Downers Grove, Ill.: IVP Academic, 2008), pp. 115-30.

where the suffering, as horrible as it is, is bad enough that a perfectly good God wouldn't necessarily prevent it is not to say that anything goes and no amount of suffering would be too much. It's just to say we have yet to reach that point. So denying the intractability of the problem of evil as things currently stand doesn't necessarily implicate one in embracing a faith that's nonfalsifiable.

Flew is concerned with the equation of goodness and being, originally deriving from the teachings of Plato. For one like Gottfried Leibniz, Flew says, used this equation to derive a system of ethics on theistic foundations that's irremediably arbitrary where things not at all recognizably good are to be called good anyway. This is the notorious challenge of voluntarism that issues from the Euthyphro dilemma. But it's interesting to note that Flew neglects the possibility that's played the considerably bigger role in the history of Christian thought based on the equation of, or at least close ontological connection between, being and goodness: a theistic natural law, where morality, though dependent on God, as the moral argument would suggest, is nonetheless far from arbitrary. To the contrary, its stability is rooted in God's unchanging and perfect character. For that matter, sophisticated versions of divine command theory in recent years, like that of Robert Adams, also nicely avoid the worst problems associated with voluntarism.[39] Adams and most recent theistic ethicists, especially since Locke, have focused on the ontological grounding of moral facts in God, not the motivational and prudential

---

[39]Robert Adams, *Finite and Infinite Goods: A Framework for Ethics* (New York: Oxford University Press, 1999). Adams offers a voluntaristic analysis of the right (moral obligation in particular) and a nonvoluntaristic analysis of the good (sounding not unlike a natural law theorist on that score). He thus salvages an element of voluntarism while avoiding the arbitrariness and vacuity objections saddling Ockhamistic voluntarism. He joins nearly all contemporary divine command theorists in offering non-Ockhamistic analyses of morality, despite its dependence on God. Flew seems largely unaware of this philosophical development and literature. Linda Trinkaus Zagzebski offers yet another possibility: a divine motivation theory of morality, again entailing the dependence of morality on God but without the problematic variant of voluntarism. See her *Divine Motivation Theory* (Cambridge: Cambridge University Press, 2004).

incentive for morality provided by divine threats. That Flew would feel the mental freedom to infer to God as the best explanation of nomological laws would make his arguing by parity of reasoning for something similar for moral laws not surprising, especially if sophisticated and palatable options to his various Euthyphro-inspired concerns are available.[40]

Proponents of the problem of evil have been steadily argued backward over the last few decades in the professional literature. Their challenge is to argue not just that there are, in principle, sufferings irreconcilable with a perfectly good God, which is surely true, but that this world features just such sufferings. The sufferings we find in this world are often horrible, but the case has yet to be made that they represent just those sufferings precluded by a perfect God. Take for example a horribly abused child who dies. If God conferred on us free will, his doing so introduced the possibility of such suffering. As tragic as it is, its possibility is hard to avoid in a world in which we're genuinely free. The world is surely worse for that suffering, but arguably overall better for our all having such freedom, with which we can do both good and evil.

This is nothing original, but my point is that the free-will defense gets us quite a bit down the road in explaining suffering in the world. By parity of reasoning, a similar argument applies to the operation of physical laws in the world. Occasional miraculous interventions are fine, but if God were to intervene every time a horrific suffering was about to happen, why would he have created a world with such freedom and stable laws in the first place? Interventions would become ubiquitous, rendering the whole venture pointless. For those who take evil seriously, here's a compelling consideration: without free

---

[40]Flew has found convincing an argument from reason and from the existence of natural causal laws, but not an argument based on the moral law. What makes this all the more interesting, since the logic of the former seems to apply to the latter, is the way C. S. Lewis explicitly argued in a parallel way both for, say, the argument from reason and the moral argument. The illustration of the parity of reasoning in Lewis can be seen in his third and fifth chapters of *Miracles*.

will, there is no real moral evil done by the hand of men. We would be inflicting suffering, but there would be no moral quality to our actions. Surely Flew is one who believes in moral evil, so he seems committed to moral freedom. By his own admission, this seems to make belief in special revelation inviting. I might interpret why this way: his commitment to moral facts and freedoms should soften him up to the moral argument for God's existence, which should lead to a rejection of Deism and to a personal God, but then the last point of philosophical resistance to the resurrection argument should be gone.

The most intractable aspect of the problem of evil that Flew seems to struggle with, and understandably so, is hell, especially if the Calvinists are right and the non-elect are doomed to go there for lives they couldn't have avoided and because of a choice of God's sovereignty alone. In the middle debate with Habermas, Flew seems to say that he thinks biblical teaching is clear that the Calvinists are exegetically right. More recently he seems to admit that there are viable Arminian interpretations of the relevant passages. Interestingly enough, Flew and I were both raised in Wesleyan Methodist homes, but I've never thought the Calvinist readings of Scripture are compelling. It's not an issue of according human freedom an exalted place, at least for one like Arminius, but understanding that God, being perfectly good, is not the author of sin, which he surely seems to be if he strictly predestines all that occurs. I know my Calvinist friends disagree with me, but on this issue I stand shoulder to shoulder with Flew. God's love must be recognizable or the claim that God is good dies the death of a thousand qualifications. And so I'd simply encourage Flew to know that there's ample justification to give an Arminian reading to the Bible, one consonant with a God of perfect and recognizable love and goodness who offers salvation to everyone through Christ. The sovereignty of God, whatever else it may mean, is the sovereignty of that sort of God. In this sense, Flew's struggle to understand not just whether God exists, but who God is, indeed raises a vital issue. The life, death and resurrection of Jesus is the clearest picture we have of who God is and what he's like.

In *The Great Divorce* C. S. Lewis shows how a man who vehemently rejects Ockhamism and Calvinism and who takes his moral convictions seriously tries making moral sense of hell, the thorniest aspect of the problem of evil. In Lewis's view, hell is reserved for those who freely reject the offer of salvation in Christ, and the suffering is less externally imposed than the logical end result of an obstinate refusal to acknowledge God as God. Hell is a self-inflicted settling for a substitute of the real thing, an emaciated and twisted version of the true good. In contrast, heaven can be enjoyed only by those who are in full fellowship with a perfect God, and that requires that God complete the process of the moral transformation of his children.[41]

So really what we have here is a cluster of related issues: God's goodness, the problem of evil, hell, human freedom. It seems circular to suggest that Flew believe the moral argument on the basis of human freedom if he thinks commitment to the latter requires special revelation. But I think he's right to see how closely connected these issues are, and I would encourage him to subject the whole package here to critical scrutiny to see its philosophical power and

---

[41]In correspondence a few years ago with Jerry Walls—author of *Hell: The Logic of Damnation* (Notre Dame, Ind.: University of Notre Dame, 1992), a book that can be read as giving philosophical rigor to Lewis's literary depiction of hell in *The Great Divorce*—Flew admitted that if he found any serious problem with his own work *The Logic of Mortality*, he would have to become some sort of Christian. In a letter dated November 29, 2005, Flew, having read Walls's book on hell, wrote to him, expressing appreciation for his defense of the doctrine, going so far as to call it "brilliant." He still seemed to struggle with his idea that the notion of life after death is incoherent, though one wonders if his movement on issues of identification and individuation where God is concerned wouldn't equally soften Flew up to a coherent vision of life after death. At any rate, what's important to stress is that Flew is quite familiar with a Lewisian vision of hell, which reconciles God's goodness with this difficult doctrine of damnation. Flew also admitted that, like Hume, the idea of eternal bliss holds no appeal for him. For a critique of Hume in this regard as well as his claim that if there is a God he must be amoral, see chapter one of Jerry L. Walls, *Heaven: The Logic of Eternal Joy* (New York: Oxford University Press, 2002).

workability. Flew can get around notions of a capricious God, an arbitrary torture-chamber hell and preprogrammed human beings by acknowledging how much better a biblical conception of God makes good moral sense, offers salvation to all and is personal and recognizably, indeed maximally, loving to all. Flew has the option to say, like Lewis, that God reserves hell only for those who with eyes wide open obstinately refuse God's grace to the end. By way of a note of interest, Conway's conception of Aristotle's God that Flew liked so much included among the listed attributes "perfect goodness."[42] Might Flew already be a hair's breadth from Christianity?

And though the problem of evil serves as evidence against theism and Christianity, it's a case that has yet to go through, especially not if the resurrection is true. If Jesus is God the Son and indeed didn't just die, but was raised from the dead, then the full range of theological significance to that event, which I've not even begun to mention here but Habermas has elaborated on to a great extent,[43] can show that in Jesus and his resurrection there's hope—and evidence—that evil has been overcome.[44]

---

[42]David Conway, *The Rediscovery of Wisdom* (London: Macmillan, 2000), p. 74.
[43]See especially his *The Risen Jesus and Future Hope* (Lanham, Md.: Rowman and Littlefield, 2003), both for an explication of the theological significance of the resurrection of Jesus and for the argument not summarized here, entitling the inference from Jesus being alive after being dead to the truth of Christianity.
[44]Thanks to John Azar, Bruce Russell, Tim McGrew, Bill Irwin, Greg Bassham, Jerry Walls, Tom Morris and Gary Habermas for helping me think these issues through. Thanks especially to Jerry and Gary for reading a draft of the chapter and offering detailed comments and suggestions.

APPENDIX

Bayes's Theorem and the Resurrection

IN THIS SHORT APPENDIX, I want to illustrate how you can use Bayes's theorem to get a rough-and-ready estimate of what you, with your background assumptions and knowledge, take to be the probability that the resurrection happened. It's an interesting little exercise that enables us to see the vital role that the assumptions we bring to our study play in shaping the final result. At the end I'll give you an easy way to check where you stand on this issue.

The present theorem itself looks a little scary, but don't lose heart. Here is one version of it:

P($h|e$&k) = [P($e|h$&k) x P($h|k$)] (numerator) / P($e|k$) (denominator)

The purpose of the formula is to calculate the probability of the resurrection in light of various relevant criteria.

P($h|e$&k) stands for the probability of the hypothesis in question in light of the evidence we have and our background knowledge. In this case we will be calculating the probability of the resurrection in light of Habermas's minimal facts and our background knowledge— our shared set of assumed facts, common sense, prevailing assumptions and so on.

The numerator on the right-hand side involves the product of the probability of Habermas's minimal facts in light of the reality of the resurrection and our background knowledge and the probability of the resurrection in light of our background knowledge alone.

The denominator on the right-hand side is the probability of the minimal facts in light of our background knowledge alone.

To perform the calculation, you need to provide three pieces of information. First, what do you consider to be the probability for finding Habermas's minimal facts if the resurrection happened and in light of your background assumptions (your knowledge of human nature and the like)? Remember the twelve facts Habermas cites and his argument for the way the resurrection would explain each one of them. Then assign a number from 0 to 1, with 0 representing impossibility and 1 absolute certainty. If you think it's 60 percent likely we would find those facts, your probability assignment for $P(e|h\&k)$ is 0.6. If 30 percent it's 0.3, and so on. Let's suppose we say it's rather likely that we'd find the evidence we have if indeed Jesus arose. Habermas has given us a number of reasons to think so. So let's say we assign a probability of 0.7 here.

Second, assign a probability to the occurrence of the resurrection on background knowledge alone. This is the $P(h|k)$ portion of the equation, and here your background assumptions will play a big role. A really confident atheist will probably suggest a very small probability, like 0.1, whereas a theist open to the possibility of such an occurrence would be hard pressed to insist that the likelihood of such an event is lower than 0.5. For presumably if God exists and wishes to do such a thing, he can. For argument's sake, let's say we assign this a probability of 0.3.

Now multiply those two numbers together. Yours may be different, but our hypothetical numbers were 0.7 and 0.3. Multiplied, they yield 0.21. That's the value of the numerator.

Third, you need to assign the probability of finding the evidence we see if the resurrection didn't happen. Maybe it's the swoon theory, hallucination theory or some combination of naturalistic hypotheses that explains the evidence, but we need to identify the likelihood that we would have the evidence we have, Habermas's minimal facts, once the resurrection is excluded from the pool of candidates. Here again background assumptions play a huge role, because a committed naturalist tends to have a towering confidence in naturalistic explanations. So even if he can't exactly stipulate a very plausible explanation of all the relevant facts, his confidence in some such theory remains strong to account for the evidence, maybe even something like 0.9. Habermas would instead likely consider the best such theory very unlikely, maybe 0.1. Let's for fun split the difference, erring slightly on the side of the atheist, and say 0.6, which seems to be a way to both acknowledge the confidence of the atheists and the challenges such theories face.

Now, we already have the value of our numerator, and we have to figure out the value to the denominator, and this third figure we just assigned will play a role there. Recall that the denominator looks like this: $P(e|k)$. Again, this stands for the probability of the evidence, given background knowledge alone. This involves the idea of the probability of seeing the evidence we see whether or not the resurrection is true. So it involves two considerations. The first is the probability of observing the evidence, assuming the resurrection. The second consideration is the probability of observing the evidence, assuming the resurrection didn't happen. By adding these two items together, we achieve the desired result. The first item, fortunately, is something we already have: the value of the numerator: in our case 0.21. The second item requires a reverse calculation of the top half of the theorem. We have to perform the calculations in the numerator again, this time considering all the alternative hypotheses to the resurrection.

So, again, here's where we are. The numerator is 0.21. The denominator is the sum of 0.21 and a particular product. Let's figure out that product, then add it to 0.21. $P(h|k)$ assuming the resurrection *didn't* happen is easy; it's going to be 0.3, since earlier we tentatively suggested that $P(h|k)$ if the resurrection *did* happen was 0.7.

What about $P(e|h\&k)$ if the resurrection didn't happen? That is, how likely are Habermas's minimal facts if we exclude the hypothesis of resurrection? Habermas would say it's very unlikely, whereas an atheist is likely to say it's quite high. Again, background assumptions play a big role here. Let's not adjudicate this for now; rather let's just split the difference again, erring slightly on the side of atheist, and say

0.6. So the product in the denominator is 0.3 times 0.6, or 0.18. This needs to be added to 0.21, and then we get 0.39 for our denominator. So 0.21 divided by 0.39 is? Around 0.54. This would make the resurrection about 54 percent likely, slightly more likely than not. Now, this isn't to prove anything; that would be silly. The point to the exercise, besides its being fun, is to help you see the role played by background assumptions. Now let's redo the calculations and contrast thinkers like Habermas and Flew.

First, $P(e|h\&k)$ x $P(h|k)$. Habermas would probably assign a very high probability to $P(e|h\&k)$, the likelihood of the minimal facts in light of the resurrection and background assumptions. Let's say 0.9. As a committed theist he'd be unlikely to assign much lower than 0.5 to $P(h|k)$, the probability of the resurrection in light of background assumptions alone. Let's go with 0.5, so multiplying the numerator becomes 0.45.

The denominator features 0.45 plus the product of 0.4 and the probability of the minimal facts obtaining if the resurrection didn't happen, which Habermas would doubtless consider very unlikely, perhaps even 0.2 or so. Multiplying 0.4 and 0.2, we get 0.08. Adding that to 0.45, we get 0.53. And 0.45 divided by 0.53 would yield around an 85-percent likelihood for the resurrection.

What about Flew? Consider the numerator: $P(e|h\&k)$ x $P(h|k)$. Flew would probably assign a fairly high probability to $P(e|h\&k)$, the likelihood of the minimal facts in light of the resurrection and background assumptions. Not as high as Habermas, though, since Flew's background assumptions stand in tension with resurrection. Let's say 0.6. As a theist but a Deist who doesn't believe in special revelation, he'd be unlikely to assign much higher than 0.5 to $P(h|k)$, the probability of the resurrection in light of background assumptions alone. Probably far below that, like 0.2. Multiplying 0.2 and 0.6, we get 0.12.

The denominator features 0.12 plus the product of 0.8 and the probability of the minimal facts obtaining if the resurrection didn't happen, which Flew would doubtless consider very likely, perhaps even 0.9 or so. Multiplying 0.8 and 0.9, we get 0.72. Adding that to 0.12, we get 0.84. And 0.12 divided by 0.84 would yield less than a 15-percent likelihood for the resurrection.

I'm speaking neither for Flew nor for Habermas here, just taking a stab at where they might come out in an effort to show the difference that initial probability assignments make.

Hopefully you can see how important one's background assumptions are in these calculations, especially one's confidence or lack of it in naturalism to provide all the needed explanations. If you want to do the calculation for yourself, follow this procedure:

Stipulate the likelihood of the minimal facts if the resurrection happened and in light of your background assumptions. (Most should put this fairly high, between 0.4 and 0.9.) Call this value A.

Stipulate the likelihood of the resurrection on your background assumptions alone. (If you're an atheist, you're probably going to hover below 0.5, and if you're a theist, you'll probably hover at or above it.) Call this value B.

Stipulate the likelihood of Habermas's minimal facts, assuming the resurrection didn't happen. (If you're convinced by Habermas's argument that the alternate explanations are woefully weak, you'll probably come in low, maybe around 0.1 or 0.2. If you have tremendous confidence that naturalism will provide the right explanation, you'll probably end up high, maybe 0.8 or so.) Call this value C.

Next, multiply A and B. Write that number down, and call it D. Next, subtract A from 1 (for example, if A is 0.3, then 1 minus 0.3 equals 0.7). Call that resulting number E. Now multiply E and C. Write that number down, and call it F. Next, add D and F, and call that G. Finally, divide D by G. That's your answer.

A Select Bibliography

Allison, Dale. *Resurrecting Jesus: The Earliest Christian Tradition and Its Interpreters*. New York: T & T Clark, 2005.

Beckwith, Francis J. *David Hume's Argument Against Miracles: A Critical Analysis*. Lanham, Md.: University Press of America, 1989.

—————. "History and Miracles." In *In Defense of Miracles: A Comprehensive Case for God's Actions in History*. Edited by Douglas R. Geivett and Gary R. Habermas, pp. 86-98. Downers Grove, Ill.: InterVarsity Press, 1997.

Brown, Colin. *Miracles and the Critical Mind*. Grand Rapids: Eerdmans, 1984.

Bynum, Caroline Walker. *The Resurrection of the Body in Western Christianity, 200-1336*. New York: Columbia University Press, 1995.

Copan, Paul, ed. *Will the Real Jesus Please Stand Up? A Debate Between William Lane Craig and John Dominic Crossan*. Grand Rapids: Baker, 1998.

Copan, Paul, and Ronald K. Tacelli, eds. *Jesus' Resurrection: Fact or Figment? A Debate between William Lane Craig and Gerd Lüdemann*. Downers Grove, Ill.: InterVarsity Press, 2000.

Craig, William Lane. *Assessing the New Testament Evidence for the Historicity of the Resurrection of Jesus*. Lewiston, N.Y.: Mellen, 1989.

—————. *The Historical Argument for the Resurrection of Jesus During the Deist Controversy*. Lewiston, N.Y.: Mellen, 1985.

—————. *The Son Rises: Historical Evidence for the Resurrection of Jesus*. Chicago: Moody Press, 1981.

Davis, Stephen T. *Risen Indeed: Making Sense of the Resurrection*. Grand Rapids: Eerdmans, 1993.

Davis, Stephen T., Daniel Kendall and Gerald O'Collins. *The Resurrection: An Interdisciplinary Symposium on the Resurrection of Jesus*.

New York: Oxford University Press, 1997.

D'Costa, Gavin, ed. *Resurrection Reconsidered.* Oxford: Oneworld, 1996.

Flew, Antony. *God and Philosophy.* Amherst, N.Y.: Prometheus, 2005.

————. "Miracles." In *Encyclopedia of Philosophy.* Edited by Paul Edwards, pp. 346-53. New York: Macmillan, 1967.

————. "Neo-Humean Arguments about the Miraculous." In *In Defense of Miracles: A Comprehensive Case for God's Actions in History.* Edited by Douglas R. Geivett and Gary R. Habermas, pp. 45-57. Downers Grove, Ill.: InterVarsity Press, 1997.

————. "Scientific versus Historical Evidence." In *Miracles.* Edited by Richard Swinburne, pp. 97-102. New York: Macmillan, 1989.

Flew, Antony, with Roy Abraham Varghese. *There Is a God: How the World's Most Notorious Atheist Changed His Mind.* New York: HarperCollins, 2007.

Fuller, Reginald H. *The Formation of the Resurrection Narratives.* New York: Macmillan, 1980.

Geisler, Norman L. "Miracles and the Modern Mind." In *In Defense of Miracles: A Comprehensive Case for God's Actions in History.* Edited by Douglas R. Geivett and Gary R. Habermas, pp. 73-85. Downers Grove, Ill.: InterVarsity Press, 1997.

————. *Miracles and the Modern Mind: A Defense of Biblical Miracles.* Grand Rapids: Baker, 1992.

Geivett, R. Douglas, and Gary R. Habermas, eds. *In Defense of Miracles: A Comprehensive Case for God's Actions in History.* Downers Grove, Ill.: InterVarsity Press, 1997.

Habermas, Gary R. "Did Jesus Perform Miracles?" In *Jesus Under Fire: Modern Scholarship Reinvents the Historical Jesus.* Edited by Michael J. Wilkins and J. P. Moreland. Grand Rapids: Zondervan, 1995.

————. "Experiences of the Risen Jesus: The Foundational Historical Issue in the Early Proclamation of the Resurrection." *Dialog, A Journal of Theology* 45 (2006): 289-98.

————. *The Historical Jesus: Ancient Evidence for the Life of Christ.* Joplin, Mo.: College Press, 1996.

————. "The Late Twentieth-Century Resurgence of Naturalistic Responses to Jesus' Resurrection." *Trinity Journal*, new series, 22 (2001): 179-96.

————. "Mapping the Recent Trend toward the Bodily Resurrection Appearances of Jesus in Light of other Prominent Critical Position." In *The Resurrection of Jesus: John Dominic Crossan and N. T. Wright in Dialogue.* Edited by Robert B. Stewart, pp. 78-92. Minneapolis: Fortress, 2006.

————. *The Resurrection: Heart of New Testament Doctrine.* Joplin, Mo.: College Press, 2000.

————. *The Resurrection: Heart of the Christian Life.* Joplin, Mo.: College Press, 2000.

————. "Resurrection Research from 1975 to the Present: What Are Critical Scholars Saying?" *Journal for the Study of the Historical Jesus* 3 (June 2005): 135-53.

————. *The Risen Jesus and Future Hope.* Lanham, Md.: Rowman and Littlefield, 2003.

Habermas, Gary R., and Antony Flew. *Did Jesus Rise from the Dead? The Resurrection Debate.* Edited by Terry L. Miethe. San Francisco: Harper and Row, 1987.

————. *Resurrected? An Atheist and Theist Dialogue.* Edited by John Ankerberg. Lanham, Md.: Rowman and Littlefield, 2005.

Habermas, Gary R., and Michael R. Licona. *The Case for the Resurrection of Jesus.* Grand Rapids: Kregel, 2004.

Hume, David. "Of Miracles." In *In Defense of Miracles: A Comprehensive Case for God's Actions in History.* Edited by Douglas R. Geivett and Gary R. Habermas, pp. 29-44. Downers Grove, Ill.: InterVarsity Press, 1997.

Jaki, Stanley L. *Miracles and Physics.* Front Royal, Va.: Christendom, 1989.

Lapide, Pinchas. *The Resurrection of Jesus: A Jewish Perspective.* Minneapolis: Augsberg, 1983.

Lewis, C. S. *Miracles: A Preliminary Study.* New York: Macmillan, 1960.

Longenecker, Richard N., ed. *Life in the Face of Death: The Resurrection Message of the New Testament.* Grand Rapids: Eerdmans, 1998.

Lorenzen, Thorwald. *Resurrection and Discipleship: Interpretive Models, Biblical Reflections, Theological Consequences.* Maryknoll, N.Y.: Orbis, 1995.

Lüdemann, Gerd. *The Resurrection: History, Experience, Theology.* Minneapolis: Fortress, 1994.

Marxsen, Willi. *Jesus and Easter: Did God Raise the Historical Jesus from the Dead?* Nashville: Abingdon, 1990.

Mavrodes, George I. "David Hume and the Probability of Miracles." *International Journal for Philosophy of Religion* 43 (1998): 167-82.

Montgomery, John Warwick. *The Shape of the Past: A Christian Response to Secular Philosophies of History.* Minneapolis: Bethany, 1975.

———. *Where Is History Going?* Grand Rapids: Zondervan, 1969.

Nowell-Smith, Patrick. "Miracles." In *New Essays in Philosophical Theology.* Edited by Antony Flew and Alasdair MacIntyre, pp. 251-53. New York: Macmillan, 1955.

Perkins, Pheme. *Resurrection: New Testament Witness and Contemporary Reflection.* Garden City, N.Y.: Doubleday, 1984.

Peters, Ted, Robert John Russell and Michael Welker, eds. *Resurrection: Theological and Scientific Assessments.* Grand Rapids: Eerdmans, 2002.

Purtill, Richard L. "Miracles: What If They Happen?" In *The Resurrection of Jesus: John Dominic Crossan and N. T. Wright in Dialogue.* Edited by Robert B. Stewart, pp. 189-205. Minneapolis: Fortress, 2006.

———. "Proofs of Miracles and Miracles as Proofs." *Christian Scholar's Review* 6 (1976): 39-51.

Schaaffs, Werner. *Theology, Physics, and Miracles.* Translated by Richard L. Renfield. Washington, D.C.: Canon, 1974.

Stewart, Robert B., ed. *The Resurrection of Jesus: John Dominic Crossan and N. T. Wright in Dialogue.* Minneapolis: Fortress, 2006.

Swinburne, Richard. *The Concept of Miracle.* London: Macmillan, 1970.

——. *The Resurrection of God Incarnate.* New York: Oxford University Press, 2003.

——, ed. *Miracles.* New York: Macmillan, 1989.

Twelftree, Graham H. *Jesus the Miracle Worker: A Historical and Theological Study.* Downers Grove, Ill.: InterVarsity Press, 1999.

Vermes, Geza. *The Resurrection.* London: Penguin, 2008.

Wedderburn, A. J. M. *Beyond Resurrection.* Peabody, Mass.: Hendrickson, 1999.

Wright, N. T. *The Resurrection of the Son of God.* Minneapolis: Fortress, 2003.

Index

VERITAS · *Books*

FROM INTERVARSITY PRESS

As a partnership between The Veritas Forum and InterVarsity Press, Veritas Books connect the pursuit of knowledge with the deepest questions of life and truth. Established and emerging Christian thinkers grapple with challenging issues, offering academically rigorous and responsible scholarship that contributes to current and ongoing discussions in the university world. Veritas Books are written in the spirit of genuine dialogue, addressing particular academic disciplines as well as topics of broad interest for the intellectually curious and inquiring. In embodying the values, purposes and mission of The Veritas Forum, Veritas Books provide thoughtful, confessional Christian engagement with world-shaping ideas, making the case for an integrated Christian worldview and moving readers toward a clearer understanding of ultimate truth.

www.veritas.org/books

Finding God at Harvard: Spiritual Journeys of Thinking Christians
edited by Kelly Monroe Kullberg

Finding God Beyond Harvard: The Quest for Veritas
by Kelly Monroe Kullberg

*The Dawkins Delusion?: Atheist Fundamentalism
and the Denial of the Divine*
by Alister McGrath and Joanna Collicutt McGrath

*Finding Calcutta: What Mother Teresa Taught Me About
Meaningful Work and Service*
by Mary Poplin

*Did the Resurrection Happen? A Conversation with
Gary Habermas and Antony Flew*
edited by David Baggett